EXACTING CLAM No. 13 — SUMMER 2024

CONTENTS

I0641240

Front cover: "A Real Nice Clambake (for Mira)" by Tyler C. Gore. Interior photographs on pages 29 & 82 by Bradley David. Matrix poem on page 80 and drawing on page 92 by Roy Lisker.

© 2024 Sagging Meniscus Press
All Rights Reserved

ISBN: 978-1-963846-06-5

exactingclam.com

Exacting Clam is a quarterly publication from Sagging Meniscus.

Contributing Editors: Jake Goldsmith, Tomoé Hill, Kurt Luchs, Melissa McCarthy, M.J. Nicholls, Mike Silverton, Thomas Walton
Contributing Metaclamician: Christopher Boucher
Senior Editors: Jeff Chon, Elizabeth Cooperman, Tyler C. Gore, Doug Nufer
Fiction Editor: Charles Holdefer • *Poetry Editor:* Aaron Anstett • *Reviews Editor:* Jesi Bender
Assistant Editor: Rayne Haas
Executive Editor: Guillermo Stitch
Publisher: Jacob Smullyan

Jake Goldsmith

Words and Clarity

I'm almost fearful of the unwanted connotations so many words possess.

I'm not fond of, or rather I am no good at naturally following, rules for *clear* language, apparently unpretentious, not too wordy or complex. So I admit I'm, somehow, posturing and hypocritical. Yet I feel insecure about this, and I really don't think I'm speaking in some completely obtuse way nobody can understand. Some accuse me of being verbose, but I don't think my vocabulary is very elaborate or outlandish; all the words used here are common and my faults may be with clunky syntax and punctuation. It takes more effort to avoid common metaphors and allusions than to speak robotically, even if I have a problem with convoluted or pretentious metaphors.

I like words, I like words that are not just useful but aesthetically lovely, and I care enough about how I am speaking and wanting to be understood as well as I can convey to also equally disdain other words. My autism, as well as the precarious position my illnesses put me in—having to regularly engage with medical professionals—also means that clarity and a fuller understanding of how I am feeling is more important to me. So I care a lot about how I speak, and I genuinely don't think I speak in some grandiose or overly-complicated way. I find it hard to 'dumb-down' my language (as I've been told I need to do) even if I strive for clarity. I don't think it's difficult to understand what I say . . . unless I'm over-estimating others.

It's difficult to speak, and especially to explain or identify more complex subjects, without using new-fangled words and evolving vocabulary, and we are often bound within the limits of our language. Much can be said, and has been said, of the limitations of language inhibiting the development of thought or creating its own paradigm; one that can be hard to escape without the introduction of new words and thus a new understanding. Use older vocabulary, and one can appear out-of-touch, offensive (according to current social norms, rightly or wrongly), or fail to adequately describe new developments. New vocabulary is not much better: redundant words in a 're-inventing the wheel' fashion abound, new terms come into use without better definitions and obfuscate things as much as they may, sometimes, bring clarity with the coinage of a pithy phrase, or intuitive description for a contemporary event or concept.

The fault of older language can be more obvious, and when older words fall into disuse or fail to properly account for how things have progressed, new words can be useful—at least if the apparent replacement is a robust or accurate descriptor, though many new words and terms are not good as acute or even obtuse descriptors. My distaste for them can be practical, suggesting that a fashionable phrase doesn't actually give a useful definition. The other concern is how so many words are *shibboleths* or in-group signifiers, whose use comes with a great amount of social and cultural baggage. Words are often over-used by different groups with different definitions, many of them ignorant or vulgar. Political vocabulary suffers the worst fate, with too many individual, idiosyncratic, and particular understandings of words by different allegiances, coloured by their prejudices and ideological hankerings. The introduction of so many superfluous words and the technology to facilitate them produce more misunderstanding than coherence. Words are now less standardised; a greater democracy of meaning occurs with words and the reportage of events with the quantitative expansion of media. One can suggest some, perhaps obvious, moral and practical advantages to advances in literacy. The unintended consequences mean that lies spread faster than truth, with this trend only becoming exaggerated with social media and the internet. An abundance of knowledge, and new words, does not mean we are adept in classifying, understanding, and using them. A larger, disorganised library is worse than a smaller but organised one.

Even when words are accurate, they can simply be embarrassing in how they sound or how they're used. I don't want to use words that make me cringe because of how aesthetically displeasing they are, which might seem vain, but I'm not just being petty. Ugly words aren't bad just because they look and sound bad in some artistic sense; their ugliness creates new connotations, their use by particular people or groups creates new connotations too, and eventually the words devolve into clichés and lose meaning in this process—thus becoming less useful or accurate.

Social classes and cultural groups use their own vocabularies and have a great selection of choice words, often adapted and adopted popularly outside their origins. I have a problem with class colloquialisms from all social ranks. Upper and lower classes each use their own language which can be indecipherable to outsiders, and outsiders are then mocked and even punished for failing to understand—if they even had the capacity to do so. This is worse when it's top-down, with cultural elites deriding those they think beneath them for a lack of education or superficial eloquence. Yet this doesn't mean lower classes don't perform a similar game, if not as socially and practically damaging. Teenagers mock out-of-touch adults for not knowing the latest cool lingo, and the reverse happens as older generations mock the youth for being ignorant of outmoded phrases and cultural signifiers. Each is guilty of their own sort of hubris. We shouldn't feel a need to mock people for not knowing what many won't even get the time to know. Why should everyone be cognisant of the latest *Fortnite* trend or events occurring years before their birth, entirely irrelevant to their everyday survival?

This is an uncharitable interpretation, and I won't in full sincerity subscribe to it, but I might define this as a sort of cultural hubris or individualist insecurity where indicating to others that one is part of a specific, insular cultural or social group is, consciously or not, more important than communicating understandably across social and cultural boundaries. I don't entirely begrudge the need, or the desire, for this cultural

membership achieved through language, and it's understandable that all of us, besides the most anti-social and misanthropic, act this way. But ideally, I would want language to function *definitionally*, to describe and explain feelings, processes, ways of being, events, etc, before it is artistic or fashionable. Which is certainly not to say words can't ever be flippant, idiomatic, or silly, but that I have a prioritisation in mind.

The use of words following cultural fashions means less care about being accessible or being understood, and this can be, though not always, somewhat selfish—and worse, creating further barriers and obstacles to understanding each other. If we don't need to really understand each other, the least we should have is an appreciation for other lives; in its worst configuration unique colloquialisms show a contempt for acknowledging the ignorance of others or making the world, as complex and increasingly fast-paced as it is, more hospitable. If a new word obfuscates our understanding of something more than it defines it effectively, then on balance it's not a good word—even if it sounds good or follows a recent trend. I think a collective coherence of words is more important than words following fashions, changing with the wind and acting as *signifiers* before, more neutrally, serving a practical function of conveying information and knowledge. Which should not be essential, but at least a decent suggestion.

This does not mean we can, or should, develop some way of speaking and writing that, in some bland, impossibly objective process, serves a pure functionality or aligns to some narrow *prescriptivism*. I am not a prescriptivist, solid in some conviction of the definition of words, and I fully accept the premise, or actuality, that the meaning of words comes more from their use and the context of their use; and I am fine to use nouns as verbs or turn adjectives into verbs, or the opposite, and frequently change the meaning and context of words in a perpetually evolving process, socially, for comedy, or just in my own idiosyncratic use. The more pertinent concern, whether or not one subscribes to a theory of linguistics where definitions and use are prescribed or described, is the efficacy of words and definitions. It is good to change the meaning of words, especially if an earlier use is less comprehensible in the light of modern understanding, and I think my overly-critical, discerning use of words doesn't mean I'm any sort of language purist. The opposite is true, I'm far closer to Lewis Carroll and *"when I use a word . . . it means just what I choose it to mean—neither more nor less"*. I'm just more pedantically concerned about the ability to be understood, or rather have my meaning not be so easily lost and confused—even if I don't think a true understanding is possible. It's a matter of survival and my good health that I express myself in a way that isn't easily misunderstood.

Trying to police and enforce language more actively with official or organised interventions will produce much greater problems and lead to significant misunderstanding, as this is an attempt to control what we can't or shouldn't artificially control. Speaking differently is not a crime. And I know my personal concerns are just that: personal, and my complaints mean little. I do not intend to be the Word Police. I'm not making a serious or practicable call to action, policy instruction or asking that others, somehow, alter their speech to fit my peculiar tastes. Nor do I, really, discredit the use of all euphemisms. And I enjoy a fun turn-of-phrase. I use eccentric or particular phrases and names all the time that others, seeking some distilled clearest version of English, would think are niche and require too much explanation or prior knowledge. I still hold some minor contention on balance that contemporary society has further proliferated, and at greater speed, words that don't, first, fulfil the purpose of providing a clear definition and eliminating misunderstandings as much as we can. Yes, better words exist.

There isn't a good way to solve this. Creating my own special and unique language and lexicon brings just as much, if not more trouble—so the very least I try to do is limit (though never eliminate) the use of esoteric jargon nouns and describe things in as straightforward a way as I can, limiting the use of euphemisms unless I'm trying to be funny or unserious.

People can be too particular about language. It's possible to say something that conforms with someone's beliefs, yet if it doesn't use perceptibly correct or fashionable slogans, or popular phrases and buzzwords, others may mistakenly believe one is not on their 'side' and become indignant. People want in-group signification and an easy confirmation of friend or enemy (a shortcut to bypass information overload), instead of a real acknowledgment of intent. The 'wrong' words are read in bad faith, and the words in themselves become more important than the ideal objective, limiting modes of expression. Words should matter less than underlying attitudes, and most do not know how to explain themselves perfectly. This is politically counterproductive and becomes a failure to recognise forever imperfect democratic allies just because they differ a bit or use a different language which people have essentialised (becoming prescriptivists).

Ideas become 'prepackaged', especially online and algorithmically. If one wants to subscribe to an idea, it is socially supposed that they also subscribe to another two apparently congruent ideas. The reality that people can, and do, pick and choose various ideas, and that ideas don't just come in pre-formed groups, is dismissed or denied. Part of this rationale exists as it's then easier to 'understand' others, and ideas generally, so when someone expresses an idea it's supposed that one can then know everything else one is supposed to think rather than realise they might only hold one view and not another. Ideas aren't always interconnected, but convenient logic suppose they are.

Some of this article is prompted by a funny post I made in an online *meme* group, insincerely, jokingly, partly as a self-parody and hinting at my own autistic, obsessive fixation with perceptions and appearances:

I hate all neologisms, buzzwords, shibboleths, euphemisms, clichés, jargon, colloquialisms, lingo, and trendy nomenclature, associated with any subculture, because I am unique and special.

Instead of using neologisms, buzzwords, shibboleths, euphemisms, clichés, jargon, colloquialisms, lingo, and trendy nomenclature, I prefer to describe and explain things with more detailed definitions while not so easily resorting to neologisms, buzzwords, shibboleths, euphemisms, clichés, jargon, colloquialisms, lingo, and trendy nomenclature that require further explanation or shared, implicit understandings others may not possess.

If I really must use any neologisms, buzzwords, shibboleths, euphemisms, clichés, jargon, colloquialisms, lingo, or trendy nomenclature, for ease, 'shorthand', or convenience, I do so in quotations and with an eye-roll (😳), sarcastically, or as a joke. This is because I am smarter than you, and better than you, and I don't wish to be associated with any groups.

Any groups that I appear to be a part of are blessed with my presence only for the purposes of research, or I am only a constituent of various taxonomical, political, social, cultural, familial, or geographical groupings involuntarily.

Regardless, that's why Joe Biden is *Goated with the sauce* and is a *Sigma Chad* with *W Rizz* for supporting the unions.

Richard Kostelanetz

Hexagrams

A poet's pencil outlasts his erasers.

Honesty unappreciated is a limited pleasure.

Dogs don't know if they're dogmatic.

Treasure pets for not talking back.

Some people lack a mother tongue.

Good truths should be well said.

A naked truth has sex appeal.

Unacceptably radical thoughts energize a thinker.

The heart's beat counts human time.

The future's the past understood backwards.

The "extra mile" is never crowded.

In snowstorms a snowflake goes unnoticed.

Consider icebergs to represent permanent waves.

Every good book leads to another.

Previously owned books often contain surprises.

Strong poems become machines for remembering.

Will you, won't you, will you?

Jack Foley

YEATS 2024

Many years ago, I was in Cambridge, Massachusetts attending Harvard Summer School. I was more or less obsessed with the writing of William Butler Yeats, and I had just finished reading F.A.C. Wilson's book, *W.B. Yeats and Tradition*. I thought Wilson had little talent as a literary critic, but he had been allowed access to Yeats' library and the quotations in the book were fascinating. I was going on about some of my discoveries to a friend, who suddenly said, "You sound like Paul de Man." I said, "Who is Paul de Man?" My friend told me about his brilliant teacher. Later, I studied with Paul de Man at Cornell University. When the notion of "Deconstruction" began to become fashionable in literary circles, I realized that de Man's view of Yeats—considerably at odds with the views of Yeats scholars—fit very well with his interest in Deconstruction. Yeats has been a presence—not necessarily an influence but a presence—in my work since that conversation in which I found out who Paul de Man was. What follows is perhaps the best of the articles I have written about Yeats.

Part of what fascinates me about Yeats is that his work became—rightly—immensely famous but, I believe, at the expense of being understood. The groundwork laid by Richard Ellmann in 1948 was immediately accepted and continues to this day, but it contains some serious misreadings of central poems. (Paul de Man remarked to me that he thought Ellmann's work was "bad biography and bad criticism.") I think what Ellmann wrote was taken up with considerable relief because no one wanted to deal with Yeats' many esoteric influences—with the highly prolific Madame Blavatsky, for instance. Here was one of "ours," a good academic rather than a religious fanatic, who took care of all that, who elucidated Yeats' complex, quasi-religious symbol system with great clarity. When Paul de Man implicitly challenged Ellmann's readings, he was immediately vilified by the Yeats industry. Two personal examples: Thomas Parkinson, who wrote two books on Yeats, said to me, "I wish Paul de Man had never written about Yeats." After F.D. Reeve and I had done a joint reading,

we began to strike up a friendship and were writing back and forth. Encouraged, I sent him some of what I had to say about Yeats. He immediately ended all communication with me.

William Butler Yeats, The Tower: A Facsimile Edition (Scribner)

I say to the musicians: 'Lose my words in patterns of sound as the name of God is lost in Arabian arabesques. They are a secret between the singers, myself, yourselves . . .'

—W.B. Yeats, introduction to *King of the Great Clock Tower*, quoted in F.A.C. Wilson, *W.B. Yeats and Tradition*

In 1928—the year he turned 63—the world-famous poet William Butler Yeats published a slim, beautifully produced volume called *The Tower*. Yeats had received the Nobel Prize in 1923, and the book was awaited with considerable anticipation. The book's title referred explicitly to "Thoor Ballylee," a derelict Norman stone tower located near Coole Park, the estate owned by Yeats' friend Lady Gregory. Yeats had purchased Thoor Ballylee in 1917. After the tower was restored, it became a summer home for himself and his wife, Georgie Hyde-Lees. T. Sturge-Moore's beautiful image on the cover of *The Tower* shows Thoor Ballylee reflected in the still water below it. The image suggests both Yeats' poetic self-reflection—the meditative quality of his verse—and the hermetic tag, "As above, so below."

The Tower contains some of what were to be the poet's most famous, most explicated poems: "Sailing to Byzantium," the title poem, "Meditations in Time of Civil War," "Nineteen Hundred and Nineteen," "Leda and the Swan," and—last but far from least—"Among School Children." Yeats critic M.L. Rosenthal called *The Tower* "Yeats' finest single volume," and the book became, Brenda Maddox tells us in *Yeats's Ghosts: The Secret Life of W.B. Yeats*, the poet's "first bestseller." Yeats himself was very pleased with *The Tower*'s reception. He wrote Lady Gregory that "*Tower* is receiving great favour. Perhaps the reviewers know that I am so ill that I can be commended without future inconvenience . . . Even the Catholic Press is enthusiastic." And he told Olivia Shakespear, "*The Tower* is a great success, two thousand copies in the first month, much the largest sale I have ever had . . ."

Seventy-six years after the first publication of *The Tower*, Scribner's has come out with a facsimile edition with an introduction and two sets of notes by Yeats scholar Richard J. Finneran. (Finneran has supplied us with notes to Yeats' notes as well as notes to the poems themselves.) What can this new volume tell us about Yeats? Are any new insights possible in the case of a poet who has been the subject of so much intense critical scrutiny?

The book opens with the famous opening line of "Sailing to Byzantium"—"That is no country for old men. The young . . ."—and those two terms, "old men," "the young," reverberate throughout the volume. In the very next poem, "The Tower," the poet tells us that, though he is afflicted by "Decrepit age," he is nevertheless in some sense "younger" than he has ever been:

> Never had I more
> Excited, passionate, fantastical
> Imagination, nor an ear and eye
> That more expected the impossible—
> No, not in boyhood when with rod and fly, Or the
>   humbler worm, I climbed Ben Bulben's
>   back . . .

Recent biographers have pointed out Yeats' none-too-circumspect, extremely problematical philandering as he aged. Is the combination of "Decrepit age" and violent youth—"Excited, passionate, fantastical / Imagination"—to some degree an indication, even an exploration, of that philandering? "With the easy chauvinism of his time," Brenda Maddox writes,

> [Yeats] used his wife as business manager, nurse, real estate agent, hostess, editor, literary agent, and proofreader while allowing his sexual interests to drift elsewhere. One of his first affairs was with Dolly (Dorothy) Travers-Smith, an artist and scene-painter for the Abbey and the daughter of the automatic-writing medium Hester Travers-Smith. Yeats found Dolly "slim and red-lipped." Friends were amused to watch him one day at a party at Lennox Robinson's cottage try to put her in a trance.

How does this slightly ridiculous philandering—this "faithlessness"—register in his poetry, if indeed it does at all? *The Tower* has one poem, "The Hero, The Girl, and the Fool," which ends with the lines,

> When my days that have
> From cradle run to grave
> From grave to cradle run instead;
> When thoughts that a fool
> Has wound upon a spool
> Are but loose thread, are but loose thread.
>
> When cradle and spool are past
> And I mere shade at last
> Coagulate of stuff
> Transparent like the wind,
> I think that I may find
> A faithful love, a faithful love . . .

These lines suggest that "a faithful love" is something one can find only after death. Another poem, "The Gift of Harun Al-Rashid," seems to be a transparent tribute to the poet's wife George and her mediumistic abilities:

> was it she that spoke or some great Djinn?
> I say that a Djinn spoke. A live-long hour
> She seemed the learned man and I the child;
> Truths without father came, truths that no book
> Of all the uncounted books that I have read,
> Nor thought out of her mind or mine begot,
> Self-born, high-born, and solitary truths,
> Those terrible implacable straight lines
> Drawn through the wandering vegetative
>   dream . . .

But "The Gift of Harun Al-Rashid" does not suggest that Yeats has any sexual passion for his wife. "Margot"—a poem written in 1934 but kept unseen until 1970, more than thirty years after the poet's death in 1939—is addressed to Margot Ruddock, one of various "out-of-control" women (Brenda Maddox's phrase) with whom Yeats had extra-marital affairs. It continues *The Tower*'s theme of "young" mind and "old" body:

> I
>
> All famine struck sat I, and then
> Those generous eyes on mine were cast,
> Sat like other aged men
> Dumfoundered, gazing on a past
> That appeared constructed of
> Lost opportunities to love.

II

O how can I that interest hold?
What offer to attentive eyes?
Mind grows young and body old;
When half closed her eye-lid lies
A sort of hidden glory shall
About these stooping shoulders fall.

III

The Age of Miracles renew,
Let me be loved as though still young
Or let me fancy that it's true,
When my brief final years are gone
You shall have time to turn away
And cram those open eyes with day.

Though the "tower," the central image of Yeats' book, surely has a number of implications—including the suggestion of the dwelling place of the isolated contemplative—one of its meanings is very obviously the erect phallus. We should note as well that, though Yeats and others have emphasized the historical implications of "Leda and the Swan," not only does this frankly sexual poem depict the revelation of the divine (the "marriage" of mind and matter) as a particularly violent rape: it depicts it as an extra-marital affair. The violent, history-making moment does not arise out of anything Zeus does with his wife; it arises out of his lust (however "indifferent" the god may finally be) for a young woman. Still another poem, "Owen Ahern and His Dancers," deals more or less explicitly with Yeats' "mad" infatuation with Maud Gonne's daughter, Iseult:

I did not find in any cage the woman at my side.
O but her heart would break to learn my thoughts
    are far away.

Both the figures of Leda and the swan are important images in *The Tower*. In "Among School Children" Yeats explicitly associates Maud Gonne with Leda's daughter, Helen—an association he made in many poems:

I dream of a Ledaean body . . .

For even daughters of the swan can share
Something of every paddler's heritage . . .

(Since Helen's mother is mortal, Helen/Maud Gonne is half divine—but in her beauty she takes after her mother: she has "a Ledaean body.") The swan appears again in the climactic third section of "The Tower":

              the hour
When the swan must fix his eye
Upon a fading gleam,
Float out upon a long
Last reach of glittering stream
And there sing his last song.

And in "Nineteen Hundred and Nineteen" Yeats writes,

Some moralist or mythological poet
Compares the solitary soul to a swan;
I am satisfied with that—

In both these latter passages, the swan is an emblem of the individual (or "solitary") soul. From this point of view (swan as individual soul), the multi-leveled Leda story suggests the immensely problematical attraction of the soul (swan) to matter (Leda)—an attraction Yeats refers to in "Among School Children" as a "drug" whose effects eventually cause the resulting child to "sleep, shriek, struggle to escape." In "Leda and the Swan," the encounter between soul and matter is presented in a primarily mythological/historical context rather than in the context of the individual, but the results are similarly disastrous:

A shudder in the loins engenders there
The broken wall, the burning roof and tower
And Agamemnon dead.

Swans in the context of faithfulness/unfaithfulness suggest an earlier poem which also deals with old age, "The Wild Swans at Coole"—the title poem of a volume Yeats published in 1919. "The Wild Swans at Coole," set at Lady Gregory's estate, is at once autobiographical, descriptive and visionary. An aging Yeats, remembering his youth, sees the swans "Upon the brimming water among the stones." "All's changed," he writes,

I have looked upon those brilliant creatures,
And now my heart is sore.
All's changed since I, hearing at twilight,
The first time on this shore,
The bell-beat of their wings above my head,
Trod with a lighter tread.

The swans' "hearts," he muses—as opposed to his own—"have not grown old":

Unwearied still, lover by lover,
They paddle in the cold
Companionable streams or climb the air;
Their hearts have not grown old;
Passion or conquest, wander where they will,
Attend upon them still.

The swans present an image of "a faithful love," one which maintains its allegiance to the divine.[1] Yeats himself, on the other hand, has become increasing involved in the beautiful "wood of matter" which surrounds him—"The trees are in their autumn beauty, / The woodland paths are dry"—and, as a consequence, has moved further away from the divine. Here too he is "faithless."

As Paul de Man was the first to notice, shining through Yeats' naturalistic "imagery" is a notion expounded by the Neoplatonist, Porphyry (232/3–ca. 305) in his *De Antro Nympharum*, a commentary on the Cave of the Nymphs episode in *The Odyssey*. Yeats knew Porphyry's essay through Thomas Taylor's widely-read translation, and he refers explicitly to it in the footnote about "the drug" in "Among School Children." He quotes extensively from the essay in "The Philosophy of Shelley's Poetry"—one of the essays collected in *Ideas of Good and Evil* (1903)—and there are unmistakable references to Porphyry in both Blake and Spenser as well as in Yeats' own work. Though Thomas Taylor "was ridiculed, even persecuted, for bringing to the attention of his age a philosophy so subversive to established values," writes Kathleen Raine in *Blake and Antiquity*,

Coleridge delighted in Taylor's works, Shelley possessed them, Keats too reflected their influence; crossing the Atlantic, they were all-important in the American Transcendentalist movement. To Emerson and Bronson Alcott Taylor was, as George Russell and his friends later called him, "the uncrowned king."

Appearing in *The Witch of Atlas, The Book of Thel,* and in the third Book of *The Faerie Queene*, the cluster of symbols discussed in Porphyry's essay is one of the key items of literary Neoplatonism.

As described by Porphyry, the Cave of the Nymphs is a kind of half-way house for all souls about to be born or about to ascend to heaven; as such it is regarded as the source of all life, which is symbolized by "waters welling everywhere." One of its gates—"the gate of generation"—leads to the earth, and the other—"the gate of ascent through death to the gods"—leads to heaven. The first is "the gate of cold and moisture"—for "cold . . . causes life in the world"—and the second is "the gate of heat and fire." If we keep only these details in mind—and Porphyry goes on to add a great many others—we can see how the Cave of the Nymphs is relevant to "The Wild Swans at Coole." The "brimming water among the stones," for example, is Yeats' equivalent to the water welling among the rocks of the cave, and the two activities of the swans—"They paddle in the cold / Companionable streams or climb the air"—represent respectively the descent of the soul into matter through the gate of cold and moisture and, since air is a purer element than water, the ascent to the divine. Yeats often imagines this ascent as proceeding in "rings" or "gyres" and as accompanied by the sound of a bell—here, "the bell-beat of their wings above my head." (Cf. the bells in "Byzantium" and "All Souls' Night.")[2]

---

[1] In *W.B. Yeats and Tradition* F.A.C. Wilson writes, "the bird is the traditional symbol for the purified soul . . . and Yeats employs it consistently in this sense. One thinks of his manuscript reference to the 'birds that I shall be like when I get out of the body' . . ." In "Meditations in Time of Civil War," the image of the "stare" is *opposed* to the image of the "honey bee." (The word "stare," which Yeats explains is the West of Ireland expression for "starling," is echoed in "Two Songs From a Play": "I saw a *staring* virgin stand . . .") Cf. "As at the loophole there, / The daws chatter and scream . . ." Footnote 2 below suggests the meaning of honey bees in "Meditations."

[2] Yeats' early poem, "The Lake Isle of Innisfree," isn't usually taken to be one of the poet's more esoteric pieces, but a number of its details—the water, the honey, the bee and its hive, the color purple, the number nine, the beans—come straight out of Porphyry. Indeed, in the context of Porphyry, the repeated lines in "Meditations in Time of Civil War"—"honey bees / Come build in the empty house of the stare"—may well be ironic, even mocking. "The sweetness of honey signifies, with theologians," writes Porphyry, "the same thing as the pleasure

Was the cluster of images in Porphyry's essay a mere "source" for Yeats—something he transformed in the course of writing his poems—or was it something else? That question is another issue raised in *The Tower*. In "Among School Children" the poet makes a careful distinction between two kinds of "images":

> Both nuns and mother worship images,
> But those the candles light are not as those
> That animate a mother's reveries,
> But keep a marble or a bronze repose.

This distinction between different kinds of "images" is no new thing in Yeats' thought. In "Symbolism in Painting," from *Ideas of Good and Evil*, he writes that "All art that is not mere story-telling, or mere portraiture, is symbolic,"

> and has the purpose of those symbolic talismans which mediaeval magicians made with complex colours and forms, and bade their patients ponder over daily, and guard with holy secrecy; for it entangles, in complex colours and forms, a part of the Divine Essence.

"If," he goes on, "you liberate a person or a landscape from the bonds of motives and their actions, causes and their effects . . . it will change under your eyes, and become a symbol of an infinite emotion, a perfected emotion, a part of the Divine Essence . . ."

The use of mere metaphor, he argues in "Symbolism in Poetry" (also from *Ideas of Good and Evil*), is not sufficient: "metaphors are not profound enough to be moving." Symbols "call down among us certain disembodied powers, whose footsteps over our hearts we call emotions . . ." Even Shakespeare is criticized:

> Shakespeare is content with emotional symbols that he may come the nearer to our sympathy, but if one is moved by Dante, or by the myth of Demeter, one is mixed into the shadow of God.

("Symbolism in Poetry")

"Shelley's poetry," Yeats insists in "The Philosophy of Shelley's Poetry," "becomes the richer, and loses something of the appearance of idle phantasy, when I remember that its images are

arising from copulation, by which Saturn, being ensnared, was castrated."

ancient symbols, and still come to visionaries in their dreams."

The "images" which "animate a mother's reveries" are in the realm of "mere story-telling, or mere portraiture"; at best, they are in the realm of metaphor. Images which "keep a marble or a bronze repose"—sacred images such as the golden bird invoked at the conclusion of "Sailing to Byzantium"—have another purpose altogether and "call down among us certain disembodied powers." Yeats' earlier poem, "The Dolls," from *Responsibilities* (1914), deals with the two kinds of images in a comic way:

> A doll in the doll-maker's house
> Looks at the cradle and bawls:
> 'That is an insult to us.'

The "oldest of all the dolls" describes the baby as "a noisy and filthy thing"; its appearance in the shop brings "disgrace" upon the dolls. Finally, the doll-maker's wife ends the poem with an apology:

> 'My dear, my dear, O dear,
> It was an accident.'

"The Dolls" demonstrates that Yeats was capable of seeing the comic side of his dilemma, but it is precisely the notion of the sacred-but-nevertheless-*embodied* (*non*abstract) *image* which allows the poet to escape from the situation he describes at the beginning of "The Tower":

> It seems that I must bid the Muse go pack,
> Choose Plato and Plotinus for a friend
> Until imagination, ear and eye,
> Can be content with argument and deal
> In abstract things; or be derided by
> A sort of battered kettle at the heel.

At the conclusion of the poem, the "learned school" in which the soul studies is not the "school" of Plato and Plotinus, with their "abstract things," but something closer to the "school" of Porphyry, with its insistence that Homer "has obscurely indicated the images of things of a more divine nature in the fiction of a fable"—its insistence that Homer was, in effect, in Yeats' terms, a Symbolist poet. Porphyry's term for Homer's sacred imagery is in fact, in Taylor's translation, "fabulous symbols"—a phrase which shows up in a horrific context when Yeats comes to write "Her Vision in the Wood." (Yeats' interest in finding a "school" is also something to be kept in mind when we arrive at "Among School Children": the title refers not only to the "children" the poet meets in Reverend Mother Philomena's Montessori school but to the poet himself, who is still looking for a proper "school." Cf. the line in "The Gift of Harun Al-Rashid," the penultimate poem of *The Tower*: "She seemed the learned man and I the child . . .")

At the conclusion of "The Tower," Yeats pours forth a number of what are for him "fabulous symbols":

> Pride, like that of the morn,
> When the headlong light is loose,
> Or that of the fabulous horn,
> Or that of the sudden shower
> When all streams are dry,
> Or that of the hour
> When the swan must fix his eye
> Upon a fading gleam,
> Float out upon a long
> Last reach of glittering stream
> And there sing his last song.

Nor is Porphyry absent from Yeats' list. The lines

> I choose upstanding men,
> That climb the streams until
> The fountain leap, and at dawn
> Drop their cast at the side
> Of dripping stone . . .

in part refer back to an earlier, nostalgic passage in the poem,

> in boyhood when with rod and fly,
> Or the humbler worm, I climbed Ben Bulben's back
> And had the livelong summer day to spend,

but both the "fountain" and the "dripping stone" (not mentioned in the earlier passage) are details from Porphyry, "fabulous symbols" which show up often in Yeats. (The "dripping stone" is equivalent to "the brimming water among the stones" in "The Wild Swans at Coole.") Here and elsewhere, Yeats is attempting, through the use of "symbols," "to liberate a person or a landscape from the bonds of motives and their actions, causes and their effects" and to allow the person or landscape to "change under your eyes."

"Among School Children" is the poem in *The Tower* which has been most explicated and, to my mind, most misunderstood. I wrote about the poem at some length in my essay, "Yeats' Poetic Art" (available from the archives of my online column, "Foley's Books," in my book, *Foley's Books*, and in *The Yeats Eliot Review*, vol. 18, no. 4, April 2002). The problem of the poem is not so much old age as it is the difficulty of distinguishing between kinds of "images." Yeats' intense infatuation with Maud Gonne's beauty (her "Ledaean body") led him to believe that she was an embodiment of the divine—a "fabulous symbol." As she ages, however, she seems anything but such an "image":

> Her present image floats into the mind—
> Did Quattrocento finger fashion it
> Hollow of cheek as though it drank the wind
> And took a mess of shadows for its meat?

Indeed, the once beautiful, "Ledaean" woman now seems, like Yeats himself, a scarecrow: "Old clothes upon old sticks to scare a bird." Not something to attract a bird like the swan but something to scare it away.

In this context, the concluding lines of the poem take on a meaning which is very different from the one which is usually ascribed to them:

> O chestnut-tree, great-rooted blossomer,
> Are you the leaf, the blossom or the bole?
> O body swayed to music, O brightening glance,
> How can we know the dancer from the dance?

Are these lines the expression of "organic unity" that critics usually take them to be? Isn't a chestnut-tree (like any tree) an expression of the ultimate unity of leaf, blossom and bole? Aren't leaf, blossom and bole parts of the whole? Are the two aspects of Maud Gonne—her divinity and her humanity—in a state of harmony or are they in conflict with one another? Aren't the dancer and the dance identical, since we can experience the dance only *through* the dancer?

A bole is "the stem or trunk of a tree." A leaf is "one of the expanded, usually green organs borne by the stem of a plant." A blossom is "the flower of a plant, esp. of one producing an edible fruit . . . *The apple tree is in blossom.*" (Definitions from *The Random House Dictionary*.) As time passes, as the tree "grows," we experience bole, leaf and blossom. But that is the point: as time passes. I think that the answer to Yeats' first question is No: his "great-rooted blossomer" is precisely not "the leaf, the blossom or the bole"— not the tree that exists in time. Rather, it is a "fabulous symbol"—something existing outside of time, or in a different temporal order from the human and the natural. The elevated tone of "great-rooted blossomer" (as opposed to the mere "blossom" of the next line) suggests the difference. The "great-rooted blossomer" is, in effect, *nothing but* a "blossomer." Unlike Maud Gonne, it never ceases to manifest the divine; it never grows old, and it constantly points to what Yeats calls in "The Gift of Harun Al-Rashid" "Self-born, high-born, and solitary truths, / Those terrible implacable straight lines / Drawn through the wandering vegetative dream."

The meaning of the chestnut image is suggested by a passage in Basho's *The Narrow Road to the Deep North*: "The chestnut is a holy tree, for the Chinese ideograph for chestnut is Tree placed directly below West, the direction of the holy land." The "great-rooted blossomer" is like those images which "keep a marble or a bronze repose." The organic tree, on the other hand, is an image like those worshiped by mothers—an image whose reflection of the divine is essentially mutable.

A similar distinction can be made between the dancer and the dance. "The dance," writes Paul de Man in "Image and Emblem in Yeats,"

> is a recurrent emblem for contact with the divine; the following early quotation describes it well: "Men who lived in a world where anything might flow and change . . . had always, as it seems, for a supreme ritual that tumultuous dance among the hills or in the depths of the woods, where unearthly ecstasy fell upon the dancers, until they seemed the gods or the god-like beasts, and felt their souls overtopping the moon; and, as some think, imaged for the first time in the world the blessed country of the gods and of the happy dead" . . . The "dancer" on the other hand . . . is associated with the symbol of the "body" and appears as a real woman in the generated world of matter, capa-

ble of giving the "pleasure of generation."

Maud Gonne may well have functioned as Yeats' Muse—and may well be to some degree responsible for some of his finest poetry. His "worship" of her physical beauty may have led him to a kind of "perfection." At the same time, however, that very quest meant that he had to abandon something—and it is that "something" which is the great issue of his later poetry. Was Yeats' interest in Maud Gonne spiritual or libidinous? What kind of "image"—what kind of "body"—has been the constant subject of his work? "Her Vision in the Wood" (from *The Winding Stair and Other Poems*, 1933) contains the heart-rending admission that the poet's attempt to become an archetype—"to liberate a person or a landscape from the bonds of motives and their actions, causes and their effects"—ends in woeful failure; the poem even contains Porphyry's significant phrase, "fabulous symbol," now not spoken in triumph but in despair:

> That thing all blood and mire, that beast-torn
>   wreck,
> Half turned and fixed a glazing eye on mine,
> And, though love's bitter-sweet had all come
>   back,
> Those bodies from a picture or a coin
> Nor saw my body fall nor heard it shriek,
> Nor knew, drunken with singing as with wine,
> That they had brought no fabulous symbol there
> But my heart's victim and its torturer.

"How can we know the dancer from the dance?" The line is not a mere piece of rhetoric but a genuine, anguished question: the burden of the poem is that Yeats has *failed to know* the answer to that question, and it has cost him dearly.

Despite his sixty years, Yeats remains at the end of "Among School Children" not a figure of wisdom but a learner—"among school children," asking questions to which he has no real answer. His stance at the end of the poem is no different than it was at the beginning: "I walk through the long schoolroom *questioning*," though it is true that our experience of the poem has deepened our sense of the importance of that questioning.

Yeats himself remarked upon the "bitterness" he found in *The Tower*; bitterness is definitely one of the volume's themes:

Death and life were not
Till man made up the whole,
Made lock, stock and barrel
Out of his bitter soul,
Aye, sun and moon and star, all . . .

("The Tower")

*

Some violent bitter man, some powerful man
Called architect and artist in, that they,
Bitter and violent men, might rear in stone
The sweetness that all longed for night and
    day . . .

What if those things the greatest of mankind,
Consider most to magnify, or to bless,
But take our greatness with our bitterness!

("Meditations in Time of Civil War")

*

All, all those gyres and cubes and midnight things
Are but a new expression of her body
Drunk with the bitter sweetness of her youth.

("The Gift of Harun Al-Rashid")

But "bitterness" and "sweetness" are merely two examples of Yeats' constantly oppositional thinking—what he calls his "continual oscillations" (quoted in F.A.C. Wilson, *W.B. Yeats and Tradition*); they correspond roughly to "this world" and "the next world." Cf. The remarkable concluding lines to "Demon and Beast" from *Michael Robartes and the Dancer* (1921):

O what a sweetness strayed
Through barren Thebaid,
Or by the Mareotic sea
When that exultant Anthony
And twice a thousand more
Starved upon the shore
And withered to a bag of bones!
What had the Caesars but their thrones?

There is perhaps an even deeper "bitterness" at work in *The Tower*. Yeats' language as he attempts to define the functioning of the symbol—the symbol "*entangles*, in complex colours and forms, a part of the Divine Essence"; symbols "*call down among us* certain disembodied powers, whose footsteps over our hearts we call emotions" (my italics)—suggests one of his primary themes: the descent of spirit into matter, often referred to in esoteric writing as "the fall of man" or "the tragedy." The many oppositions which inhabit Yeats' poetry are all versions of

this primary opposition, this "tragedy," which, Yeats argues in *The Tower*, is ultimately not worth it:[1]

Never to have lived is best, ancient writers say;
Never to have drawn the breath of life, never to
    have looked into the eye of day;
The second best's a gay goodnight and quickly
    turn away.

("From 'Oedipus at Colonus'")

*

What youthful mother, a shape upon her lap
Honey of generation had betrayed,
And that must sleep, shriek, struggle to escape
As recollection or the drug decide,
Would think her son, did she but see that shape
With sixty or more winters on its head,
A compensation for the pang of his birth,
Or the uncertainty of his setting forth?

("Among School Children")

Yeats' conception of "the symbol" was in effect Porphyry's cave all over again. If the symbol could "attract" spirit to it—emulate in little the "fall of man"—it could also lead man back to the divine. But what if the symbol couldn't accomplish this? What if all that happens is merely the fall? Worse, what if the poem achieves not cosmic revelation but only self-awareness? In this context, the lines, "the tragedy began / With Homer that was a blind man" ("The Tower"), take on an added dimension. Was Homer "blind" to the consequences of his actions? If even the much-lauded "symbol" involves "the

---

[1] In *W.B. Yeats and Tradition*, F.A.C. Wilson points out that, according to Thomas Taylor, Dionysus—who shows up explicitly in *The Tower* in "Two Songs From a Play"—"is a symbol for spirit in its descent into matter." Wilson quotes Taylor:

This fall . . . is very properly represented as a cruel dismemberment and a disaster, for life in the physical world is a curse. Dionysus could stand only to lose by abandoning his true nature . . .

In falling, the soul "'becomes bound in body as in a prison.'" "The ceremony of cutting out the heart as a symbol of eventual resurrection," Wilson goes on, "dates back to Egyptian funeral rites":

When Jupiter takes the body of the slain god from the Titans and commits it into Apollo's keeping, the myth represents the rescue of the spirit of man from a merely material existence . . .

tragedy," what hope is there for literature? The first stanza of "Two Songs From a Play" concludes,

> And then did all the Muses sing
> Of Magnus Annus at the spring,
> As though God's death were but a play.

Is "God's death" not, as Yeats once hoped, a "symbolic talisman," a genuinely magical event, but merely an esthetic matter—"but a play"? Was that in fact the primary revelation of his poetry?

With *The Tower* Yeats begins a passionate exploration of his entire career which brings him finally to the perception of an intense, monumental lack of unity, to the realization of a fundamental confusion among his impulses—a confusion which is at best masked by his doctrine of oppositions. "Why should not old men be mad?" he asks in *Last Poems* (1936-1939),

> No single story would they find
> Of an unbroken happy mind,
> A finish worthy of the start.
> Young men know nothing of this sort,
> Observant old men know it well;
> And when they know what old books tell,
> And that no better can be had,
> Know why an old man should be mad.

In the introduction to *King of the Great Clock Tower* (1935), Yeats wrote, "I say to the musicians: 'Lose my words in patterns of sound as the name of God is lost in Arabian arabesques.'" The paradox of Yeats' poetry, of which he was fully aware, was that it was conceived not as self-expression but as divine song—a celebration of those "powers" which he sensed operating "behind" nature; *yet it was everywhere fueled by a transgressive and autobiographical impulse which he could not escape if he were to write the poetry at all*. This paradox is constantly present in Yeats' work, which remains tremendously exciting but which nowhere arrives at that "unity of being" for which some critics wish to praise him.

In Yeats' early work the poet is imagined as a "priest": "The arts are . . . about to take upon their shoulders the burdens that have fallen from the shoulders of priests" ("The Autumn of the Body," 1898); "We who care deeply about the arts find ourselves the priesthood of an almost forgotten faith, and we must . . . take upon ourselves the method and the fervour of a priesthood" ("Ireland and the Arts," 1901). In his later work the poet is a "wild old wicked man." Yeats' late "affairs" (not to mention his delight in "dirty stories") were, at least in part, an exploration on "the biographical level" of this lifelong spiritual paradox—a paradox which resulted both in great poetry and in a fearful spiritual enterprise which was anything but "unified":

> The intellect of man is forced to choose
> Perfection of the life, or of the work,
> Yet if it chose the second must refuse
> A heavenly mansion, raging in the dark.
>
> ("The Choice," from *The Winding Stair and Other Poems*, 1933)

*

> But Love has pitched his mansion in
> The place of excrement . . .
>
> ("Crazy Jane Talks with the Bishop," from *The Winding Stair and Other Poems*, 1933)

YEATS

evasive,
he answered questions
deceitfully
like a politician . . .
love
fades

looking
he found her dark
hair
inescapable . . .
try as he may . . .
love
fades

God
addressed him
when he was a child
assuring him
of a lifetime of visions
and endless
love
he said, "God, I will love You always"
God
fades

      for Angela Manly

Thomas Walton

Unsavory Thoughts

How Many Mt. Tamalpaises Can You Fit Inside the Guggenheim?

I think it was at the Etel Adnan exhibit at the Guggenheim that I lost it. I lost it again. Again for good. Finally. I lost it again on non-representational art. Sure, Adnan is a genius of sorts—poet, essayist, painter—but that doesn't mean her paintings succeed. I'm not sure non-representational art ever does succeed.

Liz and I were there together, and we were talking about success in the arts as we slowly spiraled up to the Kandinsky show, which was the main show, the one we were actually there to see. The Adnan show was something like an opening act. In the Guggenheim. The way you wander up the spiral gallery. For a few spins, Adnan; and then the rest, Kandinsky. Kandinsky, of course, is also non-representational. But his work is somehow different. Perhaps it's not non-representational. Perhaps it's merely abstract. They say he could hear color, Kandinsky . . . But we would get to Kandinsky when we got to Kandinsky. For now, we were winding our way through Etel Adnan.

"It's difficult," she said, "to succeed."

I agreed.

"Some things are harder than others," she said.

I agreed again.

"The long line in poetry," she said, "the personal essay, non-representational art. It's all very difficult."

I agreed, "Everything. Life is difficult. Taking out the trash is difficult. Cleaning your apartment, getting off the couch . . ."

"But what is it that makes art successful?" she said.

"You sound pretentious," I said.

"We're at the Guggenheim, for gods sakes . . . what are we supposed to talk about? It's not easy."

"No." I agreed again.

"Well what do you think, then?"

"About what?"

"What makes art successful?"

"No idea."

"Come on . . ."

"Okay, fine . . . I guess it's tricky," I said. "I always think of that Giacometti quote. Something about how his sculptures were never what he had hoped to make, but the result of failed attempts at making what he hoped to make."

"Was that the quote? That sounds like Picasso: 'I am always doing what I cannot do.'"

"I don't know. It's something like that. Anyway, it's tricky defining success in general, and especially in the arts."

"Sometimes it's enough just to finish something."

"I guess," I said. "You mean, just to have completed a project is an accomplishment in and of itself?"

"That's what I said, I think."

"Like just to have cleaned the apartment is something to be proud of."

"Sure, sort of. It seems like success is often predicated on the parameters inherent in the project. That the artist works toward. Whether the constraints they put on the work, or what they hope to get out of a work . . . Etel Adnan, for instance, is working within certain parameters, and she's playing within those parameters. And, as viewers, if we know what the parameters are, then we can see the degree to which each painting is successful."

We were looking at a painting of a mountain. There were many of these. We stepped closer. It was one of a series of colorful, abstract shapes loosely implying Mt. Tamalpais. We knew this from a placard on the wall. We hoped to be moved. It did help us to know what she was looking at, what she was, to some extent, after. This particular painting was representational. Abstract, but representational. It represented Mt. Tamalpais. We identified a sort of inherent logic in the series, different ways of seeing, or portraying, that particular mountain, Mt. Tamalpais.

"But hasn't Cezanne already done this exact thing?" I said.

"Yes," she agreed.

"And he had already done it when Adnan did it . . ."

She agreed again.

"And to great effect," I said.

And she agreed.

"I would say with great success even."

"Yes, though I don't know if Cezanne would agree. He died poor," she said, "and unappreciated by the public."

"By which I take it you mean he died a great success."

"That's one way of looking at it."

We kept looking at the paintings. We tried to just let them happen to us. To let them be. We were walking slowly past them, up the spiral hall, around the spinning museum. There must've been over fifty images of the mountain. At some point we got to one that was black and white. It was black and white like an ink painting. Like a Japanese ink painting. Like *sumi-e*. And I said, dumbly, "look." But there was no need for me to say that. She was already looking. We were in an art museum, of course she was looking. That's what we were there for. We looked for a few minutes. It was very moving. I wasn't sure why.

Adnan had died recently, just as the show opened at the Guggenheim. She died in Paris. It said so on one of the placards near the painting that was like an ink painting. We looked a few minutes longer. It wasn't the fact that she'd died that made the black and white painting so moving. At least, I didn't want to think so.

"It's not that she died," she said, reading my mind, "it's that she was alive, and while she was alive, she painted that mountain again and again."

"It's sort of meaningless in a way, isn't it? The things that obsess us."

She agreed.

"It could be anything. A mountain, an author, a celebrity, someone's death . . . the trick, I guess, is to be obsessed by something, anything."

She agreed (again).

"Success has nothing to do with it . . . even non-representational art can be obsessed with something: color, line, composition . . . it doesn't really matter what it is."

"No," she said. "I don't think it does." We looked a little longer at the ink painting. Then she said, "Let's go back to the beginning."

I agreed, and we did.

SICK BACCHUS

"Someone may have composed music after
Bach, but they didn't need to."—A.R. Ammons.

I can see that I'm ill. Full of spite, spleen, spume. I'm sure you can see it, too. I can see that I'm ill, but I can't do anything about it. I'm tired, I guess. Someone says, "I love ballet," and my stomach starts to ache. Someone at the café mentions they've signed up for a poetry class, I become nauseous. Another person is interested in joining a ceramics studio, taking lessons, renting a kiln. They say "I don't know, I just feel like *making art*." I leave the café. I can't hide my distaste. I can see that I'm ill, but I can't do anything about it.

It wasn't always like this. Or rather, it used to be less acute than this. When I was younger, and had seen less. But now I've had enough, I've seen too much, too much of the same thing. I'm bloated. I'm bloated from eating art. I'm bloated from eating bad art.

Don't get me wrong. The great art still inspires, still makes me feel alive, still enriches my life. But how much great art can there be in a world? To say nothing of a small town. A small town that thinks it's a great art town. The answer, unfortunately, is "not much." But what few works of great art that do exist are surely enough. Aren't they?

An insufficient amount of great art is not the problem. Finding great art might be a challenge, but not an insurmountable one. One simply has to return to what is great. Again and again if necessary. Find Caravaggio. If you're not in Rome, find him in a book at the library if you have to. Buy a poster of *Sick Bacchus* and hang it on the dining room wall. Look how haunted he is, how jaundiced, how perverse! Bacchus-cum-Caravaggio. Look at how he massages those grapes. How he holds them near his mouth. Will he eat them? Or just fondle them? One goes to see *Sick Bacchus* like one would go to an altar to worry over the meaning of life.

The tragedy (the illness) is not a lack of great art, but an excess of bad. A surplus of garbage that every city and town seems obsessed with producing, with overproducing. Whose idea was that? Why and to what end? This surplus of bad art has the same effect on great art that mis- and disinformation have on the truth: it desecrates and muddles, confuses, undermines and ruins.

There was a time when every town had a factory, and pubs for the workers to go to and forget themselves, to lose their money and their misery. Drunken song filled the cities. Sad, perhaps, but true. Not ideal. Not utopian. But true and tragic and rich.

Now no one works and every town is full of art galleries. Art galleries are even being put in buildings that were once factories. And no one's singing. And, of course, you can't have an empty art gallery, so you need to fill it. Fill it up with art. "We need more art!" Don't have enough art? No worries. We'll fill it with gifts, postcards, stickers, memorabilia, objectifications of whales, moose, aspen trees, space needles and Eiffel towers. We'll say it's art. No one cares. No one knows the difference.

What the hell is going on?

A hundred and fifty years ago there was one art event in the entire world, in the entire western world, at least: the Salon de Paris. Then, in response, those rejected by the Salon de Paris staged the even better Salon de Refusés, where modernism could show itself, could argue against and boldly reject the academic art that had persisted for centuries. There were essentially two ways to exhibit your art. Either through the *Académie royale de peinture et de sculpture*, or through the Salon de Refusés, which the Impressionists formed to reject (refuse) the tyranny of the Academy.

That's it. There were two Exhibitions. In the world.

Now every Duluth and Davenport has not only its arts festivals, but its museums to fill. And most of these towns have not only a Museum of Art, but a Museum of Modern Art, and a Museum of Contemporary Art (no matter that they all might show the same works at different times). My town, the town where I live, has all three of these and also a Museum of Arts and Industries, a Museum of History and Industries, a Nordic Heritage Museum, a Native American Museum, an Asian American Museum, a Museum of Pop Culture, a Flight Museum, a Fiber Arts Museum, and several others I don't have the stomach to list. We even have (and I wish I was kidding) a Museum of Museums. You might think the owners of the Museum of Museums are being ironic, but unfortunately, they're not.

I can see that I'm ill, but can't do anything about it. I'm sorry. Maybe I should take a class at the community college, or one of the dozens of privately funded non-profit art schools in my town, the town where I live. Maybe I should study pointillist painting for a few months and have my first solo show at the café on the corner, or the café down the street, or any of the hundreds of cafés in town that are always (somehow, regeneratively) full of art! Where does it all come from? When will it all stop!

Kurt Luchs

Mary Oliver, Mary Oliver

Everybody loves Mary Oliver (1935–2019). Poets love her, understanding in detail the extent of her accomplishment; and people who know little or nothing about poetry love her, because her work, while full of depths and subtleties, is unpretentious and always accessible. She is said to be the best-selling American poet of recent decades, at a time when the sales of a poetry book often appear to be inversely proportional to the talent of the author. In her universal popularity she resembles Wisława Szymborska. She could also be called the Beatles of poetry, succeeding commercially because of her obvious charms, but also due to the fact that, underneath, she really is the best of us.

I think it fair to say that, like the Beatles, her fame will only continue to grow, for the simple reason that she is wonderful and she has something we need more than ever: a deep connection with nature, love and spirit, three things frequently conjoined in her poems. Selecting a Mary Oliver poem to write about is a challenge because it's an embarrassment of riches. She lived a good long time and was quite prolific. As poet and critic James Dickey said of William Stafford, "There are poets who pour out rivers of ink, all on good poems." That certainly applies to Mary Oliver. In fact, the poem we'll be looking at here, "Bone," from her book *Why I Wake Early* (2004), didn't even make it into the final volume of selected poems issued during her lifetime, *Devotions* (2017). Nor has it been overly analyzed. You can easily find it online, as with almost all of her work. One reason I wanted to write about it, though, is that none of those web sites reproduce the poem as it appears in her book. Let's begin, shall we?

I think when she originally published the poem in the journal *Shenandoah*, it consisted of four sections, each 12 lines long in a solid block of type, left-aligned. I have no way to verify that because I don't have a copy of that issue and the older issues of the journal are not archived online. But it must be so or all of the web sites that have posted the poem would not have followed this form.

When she collected it into the book *Why I Wake Early*, she kept the four sections. Instead of the block type, however, she broke each stanza into three quatrains and centered the type. I think the quatrains are mostly to make the poem more readable and inviting. They are almost entirely unrhymed. Centering the type is something else. In a literal sense, the poem itself is about centering the consciousness around the idea of soul, even if the central point is that Oliver doesn't know what that is. I believe the centering also reflects a degree of concrete poetry, the centered poem visually more resembling the bone found on the beach and the creature in which the bone once lived.

Like so many of her best poems, this one involves an intense, transformative encounter with nature. Yet it begins with the metaphysical. The first word, "Understand"—a plea, a mission, a hope—appears to be addressed equally to the reader and to the author herself:

> Understand, I am always trying to figure out
> what the soul is,
> and where hidden,
> and what shape

The rest of the stanza introduces what she found in one of her beach rambles a week ago, "the ear bone / of a pilot whale," and speculates that the bone may be hundreds of years old. Do you have any idea what the ear bone of a pilot whale looks like? And if you found one on the beach, could you plausibly guess its age? Neither could I. So why do we accept these statements from Oliver? Because she speaks with the casual assurance and quiet authority of one who knows what she's talking about. She gained our trust years ago. When she says something, we tend to go with it.

She continues sharing her knowledge in stanza two, where we learn that the ear bone "is the part that lasts longest / in any of us, man or whale," and that in the case of the whale it is two inches long. And here is where she explicitly connects the physical with the metaphysical:

> [. . .] the soul
> might be like this
> so hard, so necessary

Stanza three begins with the end of that sentence, the end of that thought: "yet almost nothing". There are only three sentences in this poem, and the first one takes up a little more than half of it. Not coincidentally, stanza three is also where the poem turns. Here, for the first time, she brings the sea into it, "opening and shutting its wave-doors" and "unfolding over and over / its time-ridiculing roar". Up until this point she has used alliteration and assonance and an internal rhyme or two. In this stanza she continues these sound patterns and adds to them a couple of end-rhymes and near-rhymes: "me" and "sea"; "doors" and "over" and "roar". All of those "r" sounds make for a pretty convincing reproduction of the ocean's roar. In what sense is that roar "time-ridiculing"? In the sense that time marches on but the ocean is eternal, or seems so to transient creatures like us, and possibly to pilot whales.

The third and final quatrain of stanza three makes an imaginative leap into what might be called informed faith or lived truth:

> yet don't we all know, the golden sand
> is there at the bottom,
> though our eyes have never seen it,
> nor can our hands ever catch it

Having compared the ear bone of the pilot whale to the soul in that both are "so hard, so necessary / yet almost nothing", she now compares the soul to the sand on the ocean floor—even though it's invisible, we know it's there. We could also observe that the soul and the sand have both been made by the actions of something eternal. The second sentence of the poem continues into the final stanza:

> lest we would sift it down
> into fractions, and facts
> certainties
> and what the soul is [. . .]

The second sentence of the poem ends with the first line of the second quatrain of stanza four: "I believe I will never quite know." The quatrain continues, "Though I play at the edges of knowing, / truly I know / our part is not knowing". Like most mystical intuitions, this one embraces and reconciles apparent opposites, things that one might think to be mutually exclusive and contradictory, Oliver's faith in something we can't see, the soul, is balanced by a paradoxical faith in our metaphysical ignorance: we can never know exactly what the soul is. This seems to me a conscious echo of the statement by Yeats, "Man can embody truth but he cannot know it."

What is our part then? The final quatrain of the final stanza sums it up nicely but not too neatly:

> [. . .] looking, and touching, and loving,
> which is the way I walked on,
> softly,
> through the pale-pink morning light.

I think it's meaningful that only two lines in this poem consist of single words, and they're both here in stanza four, "certainties", the third line of the first quatrain, and "softly," the third line of the third and final quatrain. The hardness of certainty balances against the softness of faith. Yet, oddly, faith is not completely soft as it turns out. It can be as hard as a grain of sand or the ear bone of a pilot whale. All of those "w" sounds in the second line of the final quatrain serve as a reminder of the whale that started the poem: "which is the way I walked on". And of course one is never surprised to find Mary Oliver looking up at the morning light.

What surprises us is how readily we accept her ruminations and pronouncements, offered however tentatively, on these invisible and inchoate matters. We accept what she says because we know we are presence of one who knows. And the sign of her knowledge, ironically, is that she is a kind of poetic Socrates, quicker to say what she doesn't know. This is why we trust Mary Oliver, and also why we love her.

Kurt Luchs

Cottonwood Seeds

A million of them weigh less than three pounds.
No wonder they lift away on the wind,
miniature paratroopers buoyed by filaments
finer than a spider's web and carried
for miles in search of water.
The actual seed is barely visible
to the naked eye, yet each one contains
complete instructions for assembling
a tree that may reach a hundred feet
into the blue air, growing fast
though only lasting so long.
Chances are, if you planted one as a child
you have already outlived it.
But the leaves! The leaves are shining
green diamonds that shimmer in the slightest
breeze, their long stems giving them
unusual freedom of movement for prisoners.
Their rustling reminds me of a harem chamber,
the sound of silks on silks, flesh on flesh . . .
and now my mind is wandering
farther than any seed borne on the wind.
This image too is somehow latent
and lurking in the cottonwood seed,
worlds sleeping within worlds asleep,
tiny travelers suddenly bursting forth
by the billions to make it snow in June, in us.

Kurt Luchs

Notes of a Former Theosophical Shipping Clerk

Growing up in Wheaton, Illinois, we were surrounded by churches and religious organizations, nearly all of them Christian, and the majority of those Evangelical. You could barely throw a stone without hitting one. And if you did throw a stone, some wide-eyed Wheaton College student was bound to ask you whether you thought you were without sin. Wheaton College, of course, was and is one of the preeminent destinations of higher learning for Protestant Evangelicals. Founded by Christian abolitionists in 1860 "for Christ and His kingdom," the school later graduated Billy Graham, and still later added the Billy Graham Center to its campus. The Billy Graham Center once included, and may still include, something called "The Heaven Room," inspired by some maniac's bizarre notion of the ethereal realm.

The effects of this excess of religiosity in a small Midwestern town were largely irrelevant to a child and future adolescent. There was a little more Christ in our public-school Christmas celebrations. So what? The few of us who had been raised by agnostics or atheists didn't mind. It didn't matter to me that the town was dry (though turning water into wine was the first public miracle performed by Jesus). I was too young to drink, and nearly everyone broke that law anyway. Why should I care that Wheaton College professors had to sign a pledge to neither drink nor dance (though King David danced, according to the Psalms)?

Our parents sent us to the nearest church we could walk to, which happened to be the First Baptist Church. This was not to instill any particular belief in us—they had none—but simply to get rid of us for a few hours on Sunday morning so they could be fruitful and multiply, as the Good Book said. During the week they were busy committing adultery, like most of their neighbors.

The Baptist church services proved to be an almost total loss. The hymns were hideous, the sermons moronic, and the building itself, like almost all Baptist churches everywhere, was a monument to ugliness rivaled only by the intentional gruesomeness of their women, seemingly intended to keep anyone from making a pass at them. The one saving grace was their use of the King James Bible, then standard issue. If the metaphysics of it escaped me, the poetry did not.

Meanwhile, only two blocks away from our home was a spiritual organization having nothing to do with Christianity, except possibly of the Gnostic variety. This was the national headquarters of the Theosophical Society, "an unsectarian body of seekers after Truth" founded in 1875 by Russian spiritualist Madame H. P. Blavatsky, Colonel Henry Steel Olcott and 17 others. The 41-acre campus is named Olcott after the Civil War veteran who co-founded the Society and served as its first president until his death in 1907. The building was erected in the mid-1920s and first occupied in 1927, set amid a beautifully landscaped estate. It houses a spiritual library of 25,000 volumes, a number of them rare Sanskrit texts, along with the offices of the Theosophical Publishing House (TPH), the Quest Bookshop, and the shipping warehouse serving them both over the years.

Nearly every member of my family worked at Olcott in one capacity or another, including me. In my last two years of high school I was a shipping clerk in the publishing warehouse. After high school and an aborted attempt at college, I returned to work as a groundskeeper. The shipping clerk job gave me a crash course in theosophy and all of its roots and branches. During breaks and lunch hours I read just about everything the Society published, along with many other related volumes stocked in the Quest Bookshop.

Some of this material was already known to me. Of the thousands of books owned by my parents, quite a few were by such theosophical fellow travelers as Carl Jung, Alan Watts and Aldous Huxley. They had *The White Goddess* by Robert Graves and *Hero with a Thousand Faces* by Joseph Campbell, as well as the Tao Te Ching, the I Ching, the Bhagavad Gita, the Dhammapada, Confucius and heaven knows what else. Through my stint at the Theosophical Publishing House I encountered the official Theosophical writings of H. P. Blavatsky (unreadable), C. W. Leadbetter (crazy) and Annie Besant (sane but insipid). It turned out that the most interesting Theosophists were former Theosophists.

The list of those that got away included Jiddu Krishnamurti. He had been groomed by Leadbetter and Besant to assume the mantle of a new world teacher, until he broke with his mentors, rejected the messianic role assigned to him, and dissolved the Order of the Star in the East, the organization supporting the World Teacher Project. By the time I began working in the TPH warehouse in 1970 this rift was long forgotten. TPH had even obtained reprint rights to some of Krishnamurti's best-known works, such as *The First and Last Freedom*. After refusing the structured role planned for him, he nonetheless became a world teacher of a sort—the sort that encouraged spiritual seekers to figure things out for themselves. He taught his own version of quieting the mind, a technique found in Hinduism, Buddhism and their offshoots. This is supposed to open up a more direct, immediate perception of reality and a state of cosmic consciousness. I say it's supposed to because I wouldn't know personally. I have never been able to quiet my mind.

This aspect of Krishnamurti's teaching had an analogue in the writings of Carlos Castaneda. He often spoke of a technique called "stopping the world." His books about his apprenticeship to a Yaqui Indian sorcerer named Don Juan were also available in the Quest Bookshop. Hell, they were available everywhere. Castaneda had even made the cover of Time magazine. It's hard to believe now, when his books are so completely forgotten, but there was a time when he held tremendous sway over many American young people, including me. And not only young people but many in the literary establishment. Joyce Carol Oates was a big fan. He had presented his mysterious shamanistic tales as nonfiction, a stance he maintained to the end. Yet it is easy to see now that he was writing novels, albeit very unusual novels. If you think their fictionality invalidates their spiritual and metaphysical pre-

cepts, think again. One could argue that all of the writings behind the world's great and not-so-great religions began as fiction that was mistaken for factual reportage. Hinduism has a slight advantage here because it embraces the mythic nature of its scriptures.

I could go on discussing the books I encountered in my work at the Theosophical Society. I am a book-loving humanoid, after all, and I assume you are too or you wouldn't have read this far. But that would be leaving out the people, who were ultimately more important to my experiences there.

The director of the Theosophical Publishing House and the Quest Bookshop at the time I worked there was a man named Clarence. He was highly intelligent, good-natured and well-read. I recall a book review he wrote for a TPH newsletter where he talked admiringly about the work of French existentialist Jean-Paul Sartre. You wouldn't think the man who said "Hell is other people" would hold any attraction for the gentle souls who generally became Theosophists. However, in his review Clarence described him as "the irrepressible Sartre," a phrase that has stuck in my mind all of these years. That's one of the things I liked best about Clarence, his open-mindedness.

He was also not a bossy boss, able to manage quite effectively without putting distance and layers between himself and his employees. Nearly everyone brought their lunch to work. Rather than eat his in his office or with the other white-collar employees, Clarence would always sit with us in the warehouse. He seemed genuinely interested in what we were reading, what we were thinking. He had a loud, raucous laugh like a seal barking, and I enjoyed being able to make him laugh. The last time I saw him was some years later in 1977 at a concert at the Fermilab auditorium by the Celtic group the Chieftains. He appeared as chipper as ever, perhaps even more irrepressible than Sartre.

The senior employee in the warehouse was Harvey. He was about the same age as Clarence but a good deal less jovial. In fact, he was downright dyspeptic, a real sourpuss. Part of this could be ascribed to his marriage—he always referred to his wife as "the war department." And part of it was due to his religious differences with all the rest of us. You see, Harvey was a Mormon. What's more, he was a Mormon of rather high rank and pedigree. During the 1950s he had lived and worked in Washington, DC, on the staff of fellow Mormon Ezra Taft Benson, who served as US Secretary of Agriculture under President Eisenhower. It must have been a major comedown for Harvey, from those heady days of power and influence to working the machine that wrapped all of the TPH book orders in plastic to prepare them for shipping. He did not accept his descent gracefully. Harvey viewed the rest of us with barely concealed contempt. I think what galled him more than anything was that the Quest Bookshop and TPH stocked *The Book of Mormon* as if it were on all fours with the mystic creeds of the East and such New Age tomes as *The Aquarian Gospel of Jesus the Christ*. He was easy to offend. I once made his face turn red when I suggested that the Angel Moroni had one too many "i's" in his name.

There were two more staffers in the warehouse, brothers whom I will call Tom and Dick in honor of the Smothers Brothers. They were just a couple of years older than me, and they were both attending the nearby Catholic school, St. Benedictine College. How Catholic were they? I'd say even more Catholic than Harvey was Mormon. They not only knew the Bible, which most Catholics do not. They had also read Augustine and Aquinas. They were politically conservative Catholics, too. In their theological pantheon William F. Buckley Jr. ranked only slightly behind Jesus himself. They looked upon me as a New Age hippie at first, and understandably so. In those days my attire consisted of ragged blue jeans, a tee shirt I had imprinted with a smiley face on the front and the words "Stop Me Before I Kill Again" on the back, fringed leather boots, love beads and tinted yellow granny glasses in the manner of David Crosby. In the colder months I also sported a Mexican serape.

I amazed the hell out of Tom and Dick when they learned I liked Buckley as much as they did. I could even quote from *Quotations from Chairman Bill* because, yes, my parents had that one as well. They stopped trying to pin me down after that. Their biggest mistake was revealing that they shared Buckley's admiration for J. S. Bach (as did I). Thereafter I made a point of always referring to Bach as "the world's greatest Lutheran composer."

All things must pass, as the quiet Beatle reminded us. So did my time in the TPH warehouse. I graduated from high school, married my high school sweetheart, tried college for a year, gave up in despair of anyone there helping me learn how to write better poetry, took a job as a janitor in a Volkswagen dealership, gave that up to escape a German mechanic who had been a member of the Hitler Youth (my second such experience, believe it or not), tried and failed to be a telemarketer for the *Chicago Tribune* ("The World's Greatest Newspaper"), and finally wound up back at the Theosophical Society, only this time on the grounds crew.

One of my new coworkers was Dan, a fellow I had known in high school as a kind of Abbie Hoffman knock-off, bright, mischievous and very funny. Like Hoffman, his head was crowned with a white man's afro. By the time he reached the Theosophical grounds crew he had taken a thousand acid trips. When the Beatles did that, it led to *Sgt. Pepper* and *Abbey Road*. When Dan did it, he developed acute schizophrenia. One day he stopped coming to work because (we learned) he had been committed to a mental institution. It was just in time as far as I was concerned. He had already threatened to brain me with a shovel during one of his paranoid episodes.

Another coworker was also a high school acquaintance, Jim. It was on this job that he became my best friend, which he still is. Jim was a Da Vinci-like polymath, a genius who seemed capable of almost anything. While I didn't get to know him well in high school, we had some friends in common and I enjoyed his exploits from the sidelines. He had an interesting band, for one thing, modeled on the Mothers of Invention. That meant their act was somewhat controversial, especially for Wheaton, Illinois. He changed the name after every gig to avoid being blacklisted, though there was a certain recurrent theme for the fans to follow: Bazooka Jim and the Gums, Banana Jim and the Splits, etc. Jim played keyboards and bass. After high school he played in a professional jazz band headed by a Chicago trumpet player whose name I no longer recall. Warren something. Maybe he was a sax player at that. I grow old, I grow old, I shall wear the bottoms of my trousers rolled, as a series of Burma Shave billboards once remarked.

When we connected on the Theosophical grounds crew we had the whole day together, and we spent it in far-flung conversations about anything and everything. If the "work" became actual work, threatening to disrupt our dialogue, we would tell our boss Fritz that were going down to the pond to "check the flow." This imaginary process could take hours.

A word about Fritz. He was an elderly German man who had survived World War II, we were never told in exactly what capacity, though he did sometimes allude to the Russian front in a way that suggested firsthand experience. Just to be clear: he may have been a soldier but he was never a Nazi (my other experience with a coworker who had been in the Hitler Youth, aside from the one at the Volkswagen dealership, was at my first job as a dishwasher in a bakery run by a Pennsylvania Dutch couple). Fritz was a kindly, gentle soul who still somehow managed to possess a few traits that seemed, in a word, Germanic.

For example, the grounds crew were often called upon to dig holes. Our natural American tendency was to make them round. Fritz insisted that holes in the ground should always be square. When he said that, he would insert a "v" between the "q" and the "u," turning it into "sqvuare," and then he would draw a square in the air with his hands. It was like a scene out of *Hogan's Heroes* and never failed to amuse us. Fritz's big claim to fame as a Theosophist was that he had used holistic healing (before that phrase even existed) to what he had been told was terminal stomach cancer. He had gone on a 40-day grape fast, somewhat reminiscent of our Lord's time of temptation in the desert, and that had done the trick.

Back to Jim. Our newly planted friendship sent tendrils out in all directions and had many lifechanging results. We shared a love of the classic film comedians as well as the avant-garde comedy that was still trying to get born in our own time. I taught him about Firesign Theatre and he taught me about Frank Zappa and P. D. Q. Bach. In addition to being a gifted musician, Jim owned a Teac four-track reel-to-reel recorder, which was somewhat hard to come by in those days. He taped his own bands and occasionally cut demos and records for other musicians. He had already become an excellent producer.

I, on the other hand, was a frustrated poet who was about to give that up, along with my marriage, to start a comedy act with my three brothers. When the Luchs Brothers formed in the fall of 1975, Jim was there to handle the sound and to record our every live performance. Later he would produce our studio works, starting with our 1978 novelty single, a Sex Pistols parody called "Kill Me I'm Rotten" backed with "Losing My Lunch Over You," a nod to Alvin and the Chipmunks, among other things. Jim wrote and produced the music; the Luchs Brothers wrote the lyrics and "sang" (music historians are adamant about putting quotes around that verb). The A-side got a fair amount of coverage in the music press, while the B-side got played on Dr. Demento's syndicated show, the same venue that launched the career of "Weird Al" Yankovic. The Luchs Brothers were to face a very different fate, but that was years away. Meanwhile, Jim married our older sister, and for the brief shining length of that union he was not only a Luchs Brother but a Luchs brother-in-law.

He will always be family to me. Nor will I forget that it was the Theosophical Society that had brought us together, the same Theosophical Society on whose grounds Wheaton College students had once burned crosses in the 1920s "for Christ and His kingdom." Jim and I had a chance to return the insult in a lighthearted way when we secretly and without any permission or warning photographed the cover of "Kill Me I'm Rotten" in the basement of the Wheaton College gymnasium. It was a picture of Jim in a police uniform pointing a pistol at my head as I sat tied to a chair with a gag in my mouth. The Luchs Brothers were method actors, in their fashion. Anyway, the gun was real.

P.J. Blumenthal

Autobiographical Fragments

Unless there's magic
the end will be tragic

Body and Soul

I

I am a watcher. There are many of us. As the name implies, we watch. We watch, but you don't see us. We watch everything you can imagine and many things you cannot. Nothing happens on your frequency that we cannot see. There is nothing you do that we do not know.

If this sounds tedious, this watching, you are right—at least theoretically. Sometimes the predictability, the measurability of the events on your frequency exacerbates the task, strains our interest—at least theoretically. What seems complex to you is for us a simple quantitative calculation. We see through it all. Every kink is familiar to us. This one daydreams about doing violence; that one plays the hidden enemy; and some touch things, with one hand first then the other for fear of harm or loss of teeth or rashes or death of loved ones. Your most cherished sexual secrets: all old hat to us, your fetishes, your worship of body parts, your denials, your poisoned desires. We have seen, yes SEEN it all. All of it tiresome when grasped as mathematical conformity. Quantity pretending to diversity and complexity. Altering the base of computation by one power or two or any number of powers and we easily follow the predictable course of any convolution.

You see none of this or maybe some but rarely enough to make sense of it as we do. But you are not entirely to blame. It is the law of your frequency.

And yet, what we watch NEVER bores us when we are on duty, and we are always on duty. On the contrary, we are moved by it—to use a word that might suggest how we experience things. What we watch moves us. Literally.

It is pity that binds us to you. No self-satisfying or self-serving pity. Our pity is a force that shackles us to your frequency. We cannot leave, no matter how painful our existence. As if we were plodding along the ocean floor, the weight of the waters of your world bearing down on us heavily. That is the burden we take upon ourselves to be near you and that is how we have been living for so long that, expressed in years, you would scoff in disbelief.

We are pity's prisoners. Sounds strange? Then you have not understood yet, confusing your language with ours.

We have been away from home so long we hardly remember it. The density of your frequency has made us forget much about our origins. Sometimes we have trouble recalling why we are here. No, most of the time.

Perhaps you are wondering how this message is reaching you. Well, it is like dictation only whispered. It is the only way. Otherwise we have no common language, you and us, and you would hear none of this.

Please understand. I am an independent existence. And yet I always depend on an agent on your frequency to communicate with you.

My agent may not be aware that I exist. What I dictate he assumes are his own ideas, his own experiences. I prefer it that way—even when he calls it "divine inspiration," though such nomenclature can cause confusion.

Some imagine themselves in contact with the *other* world. As if the dead spoke through the living. Ha!

My dictation has nothing to do with any of that.

Once again: only watchers may speak through you. There are no exceptions. Other voices are neither divine nor inspired. Let's be honest. Who else would want to speak to you, really?!

Would you like to sit on the bottom of the sea conversing with the fish?

We don't either.

Watchers watch you because we have to. It is our punishment.

II

He has fallen asleep. I shall take over. This is not the first time. I fear it won't be the last. He is suffering. Sometimes I see him slouching in his chair or stretched out on his bed staring mercilessly at his hands, asking: Why? I feel pity for him and want to solace him. But he won't hear me. He is hunting for what he calls "insight" but cannot grasp it, searching for meaning but finding nothing meaningful.

Last week he made a first flirting foray at self-annihilation. I knew he wouldn't go through with it, but the fact that his despair had taken him that far . . .

He was in the bathtub, contemplating his face in a hand mirror before shaving. I recognized the disdain. I have become familiar with all his expressions. He was studying his face intensely; music streaming into the room from the record player: Beniamino Gigli singing *Nessun dorma*, his emotions amplified by that voice. Then he unscrewed the stem from the razor and removed the blade; he perused it curiously. I recognized the shadow of fear on his face. His arms sank slowly into the water. I sensed the danger, wanted to intercede, but I am helpless at such moments. I cannot interfere directly. For a while he just flirted with the danger, lightly pressing the dull edge of the blade to his wrist. I could see that he was goading himself. Then, carefully but decisively, he guided the corner of the blade to his skin, inhaled slowly and exerted pressure – ever so slightly. He twitched. A thin thread of red curled into the water, forming a fraying cloud that dispersed around his belly. He smiled briefly, as if satisfied with this small success, but he was clearly shocked. Scrupulously he placed the blade back into the razor and screwed on the stem. All was quiet. Gigli too had gone silent. He sat motionless in the tub. Then he raised his arms out of the water, balled his hands into fists and punched at the surface.

I focused my pity on him, hoping to influence him. But that is only possible when he is at peace with himself or sleeping.

I don't think he's the sort who might destroy himself, but one is never certain. Circumstances can always drive a person to unexpected fury. Still, if the flirt had really turned to an irrevocable passion, his first words to me, when he finally became aware of my presence, would have been the mute scream we know here all too well: the Horror of Recognition. That is what we call that moment of understanding when a new arrival first experiences clarity on our frequency after an act of self-inflicted violence. I have witnessed it many times, and it is always horrible. Each time I tremble with pity. I have never gotten used to it and never will. They quiver with the Horror of Recognition. No amount of pity—which flows spontaneously and amply from us—ccan fill the unbearable vacuum triggered by the Horror of Recognition. The new arrival remains an open wound long, longer than you can imagine.

We are never hopeless. We always see solutions. We only perceive moments in time that flow logically, one into another.

Self-annihilators recognize the solutions that had gone unnoticed. But that recognition comes too late. Desperately they struggle to regain the bodies abandoned, but these are on another frequency, as if at the bottom of an ocean. None return to them again. That is why we call this moment the Horror of Recognition.

III

And suddenly the pain became unbearable. Emotions emanated from me like colors refracting through a prism, so fast at first I could not identify them. Pain and joy lay side by side like lamb and lion in a paradise tableau, heat to heat. Anger raged through me. Not anger at anyone or anything but anger pure and unformed, wild and savage, yet at peace with its world, anger accrued like savings; and now it had found its proper venue, like when the north wind settles in the north, the python twines around the tree, the tiger lounges in the high grass.

Then fear surged up and I was afraid, afraid but I saw that fear too was afraid and I felt pity on fear and held it to my heart and said: "We are both afraid," and fear took its rightful place among my unruly emotions, each a master of its realm, dwelling border on border, but not just next to each other. They converged like clouds and formed terrible and awesome shapes.

I was them, these passions, and they were me. A wind gusted within me and patches of sky (or whatever it's called when clouds dissipate) became visible. A great stillness dispersed portions of joy through me. I was awake. Names, places, memories filed before me in orderly procession, each divulging its meaning, and the past became an obedient dog, and I was its master.

It's all a film, this past. All a film. A film before my eyes. Through this film I have seen everything. I have seen nothing but through this film. My loves and hates my vanities and envies. All seen through a film.

I tried to peel the film away, to set it on fire, obliterate it, but it stuck to my hands, elastic and adhesive like the threads of a spider's web, and I was the fly but also the spider that had spun the web I could not undo. And when I did tear a layer off, I found another beneath it, and my brief satisfaction soon vanished, the new film always a replica of the old. There was no end to peeling, like shedding a serpent's skin only to resurrect the film of my life.

How to peel away what I am? That was the question. How not to be what I am? How to slice away a part I was or am without mutilating the whole? Cut off my hand because I do not like my fingers? Tear out my jowls because I hate my face?

Was not this film my skin? And the hate, the anger and the envy? Were we not one? Can I cast off myself? Can I? Even if I wanted to? And where? And how? Cast what off?

O dear. What a hung-over feeling. As if I'd partied too long. And suddenly, incredibly sober

and a little sad, awakening in the morning and recalling the party is over.

Where to now? What to do? Who to ask? I open a window heavy of heart. I have never seen the sky so blue as it is today. Did it rain last night? O and the air is so crisp. The wind whispers into at my ears. Everything smells fresh. I'm alive. I think I'll go out for a walk.

IV

Once I thought I was the progeny of angels, dropped into an earthly womb to ripen and take my rightful place among the ranks of the messengers. I was one with this conviction. I hid it from the proud, the hopeless ones. It gave me courage when my courage failed. But how to explain the gap between thought and action? It was insurmountable. And so I became the Dark Angel, the fallen one, and turned my myth into a tragedy, sometimes a comedy. Dark angels see but are helpless to act, pity but unable to comfort, lust but unable to love, call out to angels without hearing a reply.

V

Hate had brought me to a place where love is imaginable only as romance. A sentence of death, or worse: exile from intimacy. I was the judge and the condemned man, or as Baudelaire says, the wound and the knife.

I called it my farewell to history, but I wondered if that were possible or had history discarded me for not finding my place in its machinery?

I sought comfort in the myth of angels, but in truth, I knew little about angels.

And then it became clear that I was not the only one living a lie. But I did not care what lies the others had fallen for. That at least is what I thought.

VI

I am planning my escape. I've been plotting it for years. For years I have been in radio contact with the liberation forces. They've explained to me meticulously how to organize it. They've revealed to me the secret of the sexual loophole and money magic, the enigma of political might. They've initiated me into the mysteries of drugs and alcohol and nutrition and explained the peculiar contradictions in the laws of universal navigation.

So goodbye. You may see me on the street for some time to come, but I will not be one of you. I shall walk among you, but you shall be as shadows to me as I have been for you. You shall not recognize me nor single me out, and yet none shall hide from me. No part of you shall be a secret to me. I see it all.

I am escaping gravity, accelerating in a maddening flight against friction. It is a war against nitrogen, oxygen and carbon which are at once prison and sustenance.

I shall leave only this trail of words behind, exhaust fumes of my struggle, poisons for the lying tongue, enemies of the planetary atmosphere, the only blessings I can give.

I cannot vanish without this goodbye. No one escapes without making it possible for others to do the same.

I am a star and by the time you read these words engraved in the firmament their light may be a million years old.

VII

The events of a long life, all at once, words on a page: harmless arrangements of phonemes and syllables, comprising so much time, so much suffering that I mistook them for eternity. The disobedient past has reached its limits, visible, its beginning and end. The once fierce, untamable forces that imbued countless images and adventures with fear have been domesticated, deflated, are barely discernible, all substance drained through a simple insight. Yes, I am the master designer of the murders. It was I. I know it now. I was the one who didn't love you. Yes, it is true. Yes, and it was I who engineered the darkness and hired assassins to destroy the light. Yes, they were following my orders, though I had forgotten. Yes, and shyness and arrogance were my slaves, and blindness my blind love, yes, and my broken-down passion was the fist and the blow. Relentlessly repentant or steadfastly wicked, begging for forgiveness or refusing it, ascetic or profligate, calling on a God of good or of evil to heal the painful wounds or cut deeper into the flesh and the heart; hopeful or hopeless, in unbroken struggle, always restless, warring against silence, doing violence to immobility, fighting what cannot be fought: war battling peace, and both attacking quiescence.

Now I am dying. You have kept your part of the bargain, and I have kept mine. No sense asking why it has taken so long. No sense asking if it should have happened this way. No sense asking why it happened at all. An insurmountable struggle has been turned into literature. A past that allowed for no escape exists no more. That yearning for liberation seems ludicrous now. Thousands of small deaths do not add up to this one. One last breath and I am done.

Olivia Gallo

Sour Lemon Candy

Translated by Kit Maude

Mariano would come around to visit us pretty regularly. He'd ring the buzzer at about nine at night and when I opened the door, there he was, in the black raincoat he always wore, a couple of magazines under his arm. We'd hug and then he'd grab me by the ankles and carry me upside down into the kitchen where Mom and Dad were laying the table. He'd shake me up and down until I went red in the face, laughing so hard I started to choke. Then mom would say, "That's enough, Mariano," and he'd set me back down and give me the magazines. I'd go into my room to read the *Hola*s he brought from Spain, flicking through images of the royal family and the homes of the rich and famous while they chatted and drank wine in the kitchen.

He was always the nicest of all my parents' friends. He had brown, curly hair and wore tortoiseshell glasses. He dressed differently from my dad and other men their age: worn jeans and sneakers mostly. He lived in a one-bedroom apartment in Almagro with his girlfriend Kari, a morose girl with a pointy nose who was at least fifteen years younger than him. Every time she came to dinner, she would come into my room afterward to give me her leftovers. Usually, she'd barely touched her food.

I went over to their house too. When my mom or dad couldn't pick me up from school, he'd volunteer. He'd arrive with his pockets full of stickers for whatever album I was trying to complete, or sour lemon candy in plastic wrappers. Sometimes he'd invite a few of my friends into the car and drive fast in zig-zags to make us laugh. We could do what we liked at his house. We'd write, "I love you, Mariano," in permanent marker on the walls and eat whatever we could find in the cupboards. We'd do gymnastics on Kari's yoga mats, he'd teach us to do handstands, somersaults and cartwheels, and we'd squabble over

who went first and then pretend to be having trouble with the moves even though we knew perfectly well how to do them. We'd pretend we were his girlfriends, and then draw lots to see who got to marry him. The chosen girl would have a napkin clipped over her face for a veil. When I heard Mariano say "I do" to one of the other girls, I'd get so angry I thought I was going to puke.

When Kari got home from work and saw the house in a mess, she'd start shouting. "Get out of here, you little monsters!" she'd cry, dragging us roughly toward the door by our elbows. Mariano tried to calm her down and they'd lock themselves in the bedroom. We'd start chuckling quietly when we heard Kari burst into tears. Then Mariano would come out a few minutes later and laugh with us. After that, Kari would call my dad and he'd come pick us up, dropping the other girls off with their angry parents; they'd had no idea where their daughters were all afternoon. One by one, said parents began forbidding them from coming over, but I didn't care. *Better this way*, I thought. *Now I'm the only one who can marry Mariano.*

A few months went by when Mariano didn't come over. We still saw Kari fairly regularly and she and Mom would huddle together in the kitchen. I'd try to put my ear to the door to listen in on their conversation but the door was thick and Kari was always breaking down. Apparently, Mariano had broken all the windows in the house and when Kari got home, she found him lying on top of the shards of glass, waving his arms like he was making a snow angel. That was exactly how she said it, "He was waving his arms like he was making a snow angel." I laughed because it was probably one of Mariano's jokes, the kind that Kari never got.

But Mom and Dad started talking about Mariano in worried tones. They told their other friends that he'd had an "episode," which made me think of a TV series. They also mentioned a clinic where they went to visit Mariano sometimes, but even though I begged and begged, they never took me with them. One day, he was released. No one told me that either, I only found out when he came over one night for dinner with Kari. He said hello, and seemed very happy to see me, but we didn't play. That night I was allowed to eat at the table with them, and Mariano barely said anything. Just yes, no, and a few other words. He smiled a lot. Kari looked as though she hadn't been sleeping well.

I barely saw him anymore, but one day he came by the house to pick me up. I was on my own when the buzzer went. I went downstairs. He was waiting in the car, the same one as before, only now the doors had dents in them. I sat in the front and as I leaned over to buckle my seatbelt I saw a pile of sour lemon candy wrappers on the floor, covered in dust. It was the first time I had ever experienced the awful, delectable feel of nostalgia in the pit of my stomach.

Mariano barely said a word on our journey. He just asked me what radio station I wanted to listen to. I said I didn't know, I never listened to the radio. He chose one at random. He didn't say where we were going, but we pulled up at a cinema. He bought tickets for a movie he chose without asking me. We were in the lobby with a tub of popcorn and a box of chocolate-covered peanuts that he poured over the popcorn. The film was for grown-ups, extremely boring. At one point, he said he had to go to the bathroom and got up. I was left alone in the theater and ate popcorn until I fell asleep. I was woken up by an usher, a teenager with rampant acne and a blue visor. The lights had come up and the screen was blank.

The usher walked me out and helped me look for Mariano. We found him on the bathroom floor, his face wet. He said he was fine, he'd just felt faint for a moment but he was OK now. He smiled and took my hand, telling me to walk faster. I turned around to see the usher watching us, scratching his forehead underneath the visor.

Mariano's hands were shaking so much that it was like they had a life of their own. He tried to stop the shaking by gripping the steering wheel hard, until his knuckles turned white. He didn't

say where we were going this time either, but I assumed he was taking me home. For the first time since I'd known him, I was hoping we'd go there instead of his house.

"I'm going to show you something you've never seen before," he said eventually. I didn't answer. He said the phrase over and over again, like he'd forgotten he'd said it. "I'm going to show you something you've never seen before," he said again, when we were in the elevator, going up to his apartment.

He made a couple of attempts to open his door, but his hand was shaking too much for him to get the key in the lock. We eventually got inside and he strode straight across the room to the balcony. I watched him from the threshold of the apartment. I didn't dare go any further. I saw him open the door and go out. That was all I saw, but I heard a loud thud from down below, followed by a flock of flustered pigeons.

A few days later, my parents and I went to visit some friends at their place in the country. I was swimming in the pool on my own, when Mom dove in head first. The others were in the house, drinking coffee after lunch. It sounded like a slap when her body hit the water. She quickly climbed back out and went to sit on a white plastic lounger. I went on swimming. I ducked under the water to see how long I could hold my breath. My mom said something and I poked my head above the surface.

"What?" I asked.

"Mariano died today," she answered.

She and Dad had been to see him in the hospital after he jumped off the balcony; a store canopy had broken the fall. He spent ten days on life support. When Mom told me, I looked at her and it felt like I was crying because my face was wet, but it might just have been the water from the pool.

TORI BOND

NECROMANCING HORATIO ALGER

Paul pried open the casket sitting on sawhorses in their two-car garage. In the silent language of couples, Nancy asked one last time if he was sure he wanted to resurrect his childhood hero.

He nodded. Nancy lit three candles on Paul's workbench. "I need a beating heart."

He stammered and scuffed a dirt clod with the toe of his AllCelebrity off-brand sneaker.

Nancy arranged amethyst, kyanite, and bloodstone crystals in a triangle and placed a tattered copy of *Ragged Dick* in the center. "I need a beating heart."

He squeamishly offered a frog he'd caught in a nearby pond.

"That'll have to do." She grabbed it, made a slit from chin to groin, and pinched out its beating heart in one swift motion.

She scared him sometimes, but he loved her take charge attitude.

"I call on Hecate to recompose Horatio's rotted composted disposition," Nancy chanted. "Grant this charmer of virtuous words permission to cross back into the world of the living so he may right ungodly wrongs."

The burning Solomon's Seal and Wormwood incense, the incantations calling on unknown forces of life and death, including, Paul feared, the Devil himself, got mixed up in a nauseous sweaty haze. Next thing Paul knew, Horatio Alger was sitting on his couch dressed in sweatpants.

Paul wrung his hands anxiously. "I've got a bone to pick with you."

Horatio looked down at his decaying body as if wondering which bone he was going to snatch. "Why am I here exactly?"

"Ragged Dick was my hero." Paul flushed with excitement.

With what little flesh he had on his face, Horatio smiled proudly.

"I believed in Dick. I wanted to be Dick. Through hard work, honesty, and pluck, he pulled himself up from boot-black . . ."

"To clerk!" Nancy had entered the house from the garage. Her hands dripped a sanguine slime. "Ragged Dick pulled himself up to an honest hard-working clerk. And that was with the help of a wealthy gent."

"He never stole or cheated anyone. He was frank and noble and frugal." Paul spit his words at Nancy, relitigating an ancient argument.

Nancy directed her words at Horatio. "Virtues smirtues. You know what that got us? Fucked. That's what, and it's all your fault." She pointed her finger at Horatio's face.

Horatio jerked away from the spit spewing from her angry mouth.

Nancy glared at Paul. "I've got packing to do." She headed for the stairs calling over her shoulder, "The sheriff is locking us out at sundown."

"I think my work here is done." Horatio attempted to stand.

"Whoa, we're not done yet." Paul paced the length of the couch. The only other furniture in the living room was a bare-bulbed lamp sitting on the floor. The rest had been burned for heat.

"Let me puzzle this out. You and your lovely wife," Horatio paused to shudder, "Nancy, acquired an ancient book of magic and the first spell you attempt is raising the dead? Why not conjure a bag of gold or a genie to grant you three wishes?"

"Are you calling me stupid?"

Horatio tried to clear his throat, but it was much too dry for that. He managed a rasping growl. "I am too much of a gentleman for name calling, sir."

Katie, Paul's ten-year-old daughter, ran down the stairs screaming, "Mommy's a witch!"

Paul hooked her arm. "Young lady, do not call your mother a bitch."

"You do."

Paul blinked.

"She did this to me!" Katie made urgent gestures around her head as if it were stuck inside an enormous ball. Her golden locks writhed and hissed. The motion of her hands excited the serpents rooted there.

Paul assured Katie that "Mother was only trying to help."

Katie gave him the finger when he wasn't looking.

A gigantic bubble floated down the stairs with Paul's son, Boyd, trapped within its iridescent roundness.

"What is Mom working on now?" Paul said.

"I told Mom that I was hungry." The bubble bounced on the ceiling.

Paul untangled three snakes from his neck.

"Ouch!" Katie smacked Paul's hand. Five more snakes wove a chain around Paul's neck.

Nancy appeared out of nowhere. "I can't make the magic work without the right ingredients."

Paul suggested Boyd eat beans from the overflowing pot in the kitchen.

"Nancy, I have agreed to do business with the Devil, but I draw the line at murder," Paul said.

"No one would miss the ShopRite bum, dear!"

"I hate beans." Boyd said.

"I love beans," Katie said. "What's wrong with beans?"

"Shut up Katie," Boyd said.

"No, you shut up!"

Nancy sat next to Horatio, placed her arm around his shoulders. "You know what our biggest problem is? My husband doesn't have the balls to procure the needed ingredients for conjuring what we need."

"I hate generic no-name food!" Boyd said.

"Really Nancy, do you really think it's necessary to air our dirty laundry in front of our guest?"

"Why can't we be like normal people and eat hamburgers and fries from Burger World or five-foot hoagies from Sub World?" Boyd said as he tumbled angrily in his bubble.

"You should be grateful you have beans to eat." Paul untangled himself from Katie's hair-snakes and escorted her out the door. "Go find some crickets? Your hair looks hungry."

"You have no idea how hard it is to make a living." It pained Paul to deny his children so much.

"Oh really? The neighbors have jobs. All my friends' parents have jobs." Boyd's bubble danced around room. "You two are just lazy. It's ruining my life!"

Paul batted the bubble toward the door. "Why don't you get a job?" He wedged it into the open doorway.

Boyd crossed his arms. "Fine. I will."

Paul kicked the bubble and was repelled backward. He then slammed his butt against it and the bubble broke loose and floated skyward.

"If you get stuck in a tree," Paul yelled, "call one of your brand-named-sandwich-eating friends to come rescue you!"

"Don't you think that was a bit harsh?" Horatio asked.

"He's just a teenager, Paul," Nancy said. It was strange for her to warm so quickly to Horatio. She never liked any of his other friends.

Paul stood in front of the pair with hands on hips. "We used to be partners. You've changed, Nancy."

Nancy jumped to her feet. "Really? You think? My vows were for sickness and health. I didn't sign up for crippling debt, home foreclosure, and long-term joblessness unless you call selling my body for food a career?" Nancy hunched like an animal ready to pounce.

Horatio inched to the far end of the couch.

Nancy's eyes locked onto Paul's, communicating her rage about fifteen years of failure and struggle, fifteen years of love transformed into a loathing hell that neither of them could escape due to their financial situation. "I am going to do something to save our family." Her gritted teeth said more than her words. "I refuse to sit by idly and watch our family disintegrate because your factory job went on vacation and never came home. *I* refuse to surrender to the kids' hunger because you spent every last penny of our savings, then borrowed even more, to learn computer programming in time to say bon voyage to the computer industry when it sailed to India." She stomped up the stairs.

"Please be careful dear," Paul called after her in a sweet voice.

Nancy turned and glared at both men. Paul stumbled backwards and landed on Horatio. There was a loud crack.

"Oh shit," Paul said.

Nancy's face tightened. "We've gone to a lot of trouble to bring him back from the dead and now you go and break him?"

Paul patted and smoothed Horatio's arms and torso. "He's fine. See. Everything's okay."

Horatio patted his legs, reached into his sweatpants and pulled out a thigh bone. "I'm fine. I'm okay. I probably don't need this."

Through gritted teeth, Nancy told Paul where to find the duct tape and she disappeared.

Paul instructed Horatio to hold his thigh bone in place while he wrapped it with tape. Horatio asked why they hadn't resurrected him whole, with all of his flesh intact.

"Sorry man. We're working on it." Paul said. "We practiced on Mr. Tibbs."

"I'd very much like to meet this distinguished Mr. Tibbs?"

Paul stuck two fingers in his mouth and whistled. A black dog, with some of its fur intact, entered the room, dragging his hind legs.

"Good God, why would you bring this poor creature back from the abyss?" Horatio tried to raise an eyebrow, but he had none.

"You know, after losing our jobs and getting the house foreclosure notice, Nancy found a lump in her breast." Paul sniffed back tears. "When Mr. Tibbs—" Paul paused and cleared his throat. "When Mr. Tibbs got hit by a car, we just couldn't accept his loss. Nancy's okay with raising the dead." He reached down and scratched Mr. Tibbs' ear causing the ear to drop off. "Her healing spells need work." Paul spoke baby talk

to the dog. "Isn't that right Mr. Tibbs? Mommy's going to fix your legs. Oh, yes she is."

Mr. Tibbs sniffed at his dislocated ear and then dragged himself out of the room.

The *shirrping* tape sounds continued. "I brought you back to life because you seemed to have all the answers. Your robust formula for a good life worked for us. We bought this house and dreamed of sending the kids to community college. We even splurged once a month and ate at one of those name-brand fast-food restaurants Boyd loves."

Something exploded upstairs. They stared at the ceiling.

"All clear," Nancy yelled.

"What does that mean Nancy?" Paul yelled at the ceiling.

She appeared at the top of the stairs smoldering, with a blackened face and burn holes in her blouse. "I'm fine—I'm fine—But the cat didn't make it."

Paul dropped his chin. "As long as you're okay, Honey."

Nancy lingered a moment as if wanting to say more, then left.

"Things used to be pretty good. But now, Nancy says I'm not the man she fell in love with."

Paul yanked a piece of tape from Horatio's leg "You got to hold the bone steady." He continued to mummify Horatio's leg. "Hell, Nancy doesn't see a man at all when she looks at me. We haven't had sex in over a year."

"That Nancy is a bit difficult to warm up to," Horatio said.

"That's my wife you're talking about."

"I didn't mean to offend. I'm just saying—she is a bit scary," Horatio said.

"I don't blame Nancy." Paul wiped his dripping nose. "I failed her. All I want is to make her happy."

Horatio placed his hand on Paul's shoulder.

"Thanks man. I appreciate your trying to comfort me, but if you don't mind," Paul politely brushed Horatio's hand from his shoulder. "Your hand smells really bad."

Horatio tucked his hand under his sweatshirt. "I feel that I have led you astray. I would very much like to help restore your fortunes."

"There's nothing you can do. I'm an idiot for bringing you back," Paul said. "I was just so mad. I needed to yell at someone."

"Don't give up, Paul. One of the most important virtues that Ragged Dick possessed was tenacity."

"That and a rich benefactor," Paul said. "Do you have any money?"

Horatio punched him playfully. His pinky fell off.

Paul winced. "Did that hurt?"

Horatio stared at the hole left by his absent digit. "Surprisingly, no."

Paul taped the pinky back on. Horatio examined his mummified hand. "I think we should rob a bank. You still have banks, don't you?"

"Ragged Dick would never rob a bank," Paul said.

"Ragged Dick lived during a time when virtues meant something. It appears that my philosophies have failed you. Let's rewrite your story, Paul. Do you have a get-away car?"

P aul waited outside the WeOwnU FederalChina Bank for a fast get-a-way, but Horatio was taking much too long. They had argued about who should "proffer" the stick-up note. Horatio won. He had less to lose if he got caught, plus security wouldn't be able to ID him, since he died long before face recognition software collected and profiled every single being on Earth via social media. Paul's frustration boiled over when he tried to explain social media to Horatio. Then he tried to explain what "high-tech Big Brother" meant and finally said, "never mind, it wasn't important." Paul got out of the car and pressed his face to the glass doors. Horatio wrestled with something at the teller's counter. Then it happened. His arms dropped off from the weight of the bag of cash. He then kicked the bag toward the door, moving it about five feet before grabbing his knee.

Paul motioned wildly for him to hurry. Horatio abandoned the bag of cash and hobbled to the door.

"What's wrong with you? Why didn't you kick the bag out the door?"

"It felt like my leg was coming loose."

"This is no time to fall apart—get in the car. Just get in the car."

Horatio apologized profusely until Paul told him to shut up. They cooked up the idea that Paul should rob a liquor store. They picked out a small place on a seedy street off Main, but Paul ultimately chickened out. Horatio reminded him that his hero, Ragged Dick, succeeded due to courage. Paul almost took his head off. "Stop with the virtues!"

"Fine," Horatio said.

After a silent ride home, Paul pulled the car into their driveway. Nancy sat on the sofa in the front lawn with their refrigerator, toilet, and a small pile of clothes.

"It looks like the sheriff has been here." Paul couldn't move.

Katie sat on the couch feeding crickets to her hair. There was no sign of Boyd. Nancy paged frantically through the book of magic.

"Where are we going to live?" Horatio expressed his worry by picking at his fingers.

Paul knew that the finger picking would not end well but held his tongue. "What are you worried about? You're dead."

"Why must you keep reminding me?

"It's the truth." Paul waited for a response, but Horatio wouldn't face him. "Okay. Fine. I'm sorry."

"I may be dead but I'm still sentient," Horatio's voice quivered.

"Sentient? You with the big words. Sheesh."

"You went to great lengths to bring me back and I have disappointed you. When I was alive, I remember how hard it was to support just myself. You have three other people to support—

plus one." Horatio sheepishly pointed to him-self. "What are you going to do, my friend?"

"I got this strange feeling, right here." Paul grabbed a handful of his belly fat. "Like I feel a little dead inside."

"Are you making a joke at my expense?" Horatio said.

Paul sniffed and swallowed hard. "No man. I'm sorry I dragged you into the middle of my problems."

Sirens blared in the distance and grew louder. "The police will be here soon," Paul said.

"I think honesty is the best policy," Horatio said. "When they get here, I will accept all re-sponsibility for the attempted theft."

"Falling on your sword isn't gonna save me. I drove the get-away car."

"Perhaps we can look for the silver lining in this situation. At least in jail we will have modest accommodations and basic meals," Horatio said.

"If it were that simple, don't you think we all would have committed heinous crimes by now? If I go to jail, they'll make Nancy pay for my keep and she is so pissed at me already."

Horatio winced.

They sat listening to the engine tick as it cooled down. Paul preferred dealing with the stench of Horatio's rotting decay than facing Nancy's rage.

Horatio let out an *eek* right before his head dropped into his lap. "Oh my," he said and stared up at Paul with a bewildered look.

"It was selfish of me to wake you from your eternal nap." Paul wanted to pat Horatio's shoul-der but was afraid something else might fall off. "You'd probably be better off dead."

"From my vantage point, I'd say being fully dead is better off than half alive."

Samson Bulkley

On The Way

In a shop whose atmosphere commanded an oppressive quiet to those that browsed its wares, a young boy dutifully followed his mother. He had wide, attentive eyes and a child-ish paunch beneath his buttoned shirt. His mother stopped at some cherub figurines and considered them with some acuity quite beyond the boy, and he continued on patterning each consideration of the store's contents with a dif-fident step across the carmine-colored carpet. He saw ornate, unmoving clocks with gold hands and hollow innards. He looked eye to eye with childsized statues. There were books bound with ornate covers that revealed nothing about their contents, but the boy did not dare to delve within their revered, flimsy pages. At the deep-est end of the store, where the walls were stacked with shelves from bottom to top, there were unreasoned divisions of objects: vintage card sets sat next to blue-printed China, a black-

amoor lamp surrounded by glinting rings, im-maculate children toys lain by an ancient, de-funct gun. He walked towards this wall and stopped suddenly. There was a man stood darkly next to those shelves. He was large, unkempt, and some fresh misery churned beneath his va-cant eyes. His name was Robert, and he saw that this boy was fresh-faced in his Sunday best. His small face was uncomfortably contorted, and he took one small step back under Robert's curious gaze. Children, he thought, are at the mercy of their emotions. Mouth slightly agape, eyes wide, the boy could not hide his discomfort and like an abandoned spike, he skidded away the moment Robert spoke to him. No point in taking it per-sonally, Robert thought. He remembered, when he was a child, shrugging uselessly under the beaming look of many a good-natured, child-loving stranger. On the other hand, he had known many people that could naturally and ef-fectively excite a child. People that drew glee from children as naturally as he drew fear. There was no denying it. It was something of himself that the child was reacting to. He decided to leave the shop without a purchase catching the child now standing in the protective umbrella of his stout mother's presence. Blond hair with densely packed curls, she met his eyes with a strain of discomfort not unlike her son's.

Outside, the sun fell unobstructed in the cool, Autumn air. He walked along the street gauging his specter in the shop windows, readjusting his shoulders, bringing his chin upward, and smoothing his hair as best as he could. Every edge seemed softened by the cool weather. The red-brown brick, the wood, the plaster, they all took less rigid shape, and the slightest stumble seemed it could bring them down into a cartoonish heap. He fought against the chill in the weather. He felt his coat beat back the cold only for the Sun to assault that hard-won recess. The beginnings of a swelter were churning in his pits and a furnace-like heat vented upward from the neck of his coat.

He came under an apartment building and stood outside its gate for a moment. Its pattern of windows and balconies were spaced across its sun-covered face. In one balcony, he saw a young, blonde woman whose clothing did not reflect the weather. Her arms and legs were nearly entirely bare. She was opalescently pale, and her limbs were long and lean. Much like her, Robert thought. He wondered if she's in the same business. It must be difficult to relax inside with so many coming in and out. She might need a moment of freedom in the Sun. Many stresses with such a life. Perhaps even considering some daring proposal made by one of her customers. Her features were made blank by the distance but her limbs were made bolder and an elongated foot stood on the bottom rail hanging out in the air. He remained there unseen hoping that she might notice him and motion him up with an adumbrated smile and a feathery flip of her fingers. What is the trick, he wondered, to such a woman? He felt the wad of money in his pocket and continued walking.

The street gave way to small, motionless homes. A lane of trees crowded the banks of the sidewalks. The cold had browned the edges of their leaves giving them the look of being consumed by a slow and silent fire. Bushes huddled before the wells of windows, and chokecherries spilled across spots of concrete in red, viscous piles. He had been here once with Mandy. She had sneered the entire walk complaining of her ankle (which he made note did not seem quite so bothersome the very next day), she snorted when he pointed out all the houses he found most charming, and she shrugged when he connected some neighborhood element to his own childhood. It's difficult, he reflected, to recall what had first made marriage seem a good idea.

When he approached the park, he had really begun to sweat. His head was sopped and a heat filled the cavities of his body with a feverish swill. Mustn't be a mess when I get there, he thought and sat on the first bench he saw. The spot was nestled deep in the unexpectedly frigid shadow of a very large elm, but he decided it would cool his body quicker if he could only endure it. He also decided Mandy had never seemed to like him. He supposed that was why the sudden and violent jealousy was so surprising. Her round face, usually so firm, was softened with a frightened rage and piteous hurt. With an endless cascade of tears that bedewed her bloated face, she had been a very pathetic and alien thing to him.

A few families trickled into the park. He tried smiling at the children and nodding at the parents. He and Mandy never had children. Her unserviceable womb and his constant ennui provided ample enough reason, but now, he felt the thought was strangely attractive. He saw a young girl wearing a purple coat over a polka dot dress. She had a wide forehead and grinned with spaced, unblemished teeth. He imagined her as his daughter, instinctually loyal, adoring, but the wholesome vision quickly gave way to a recalcitrant brat perpetually sickened by his presence, by his touch. He lamented that his mind never allowed a nice thought and that he seemed forever prone to cynicism even in his own fancies.

He tried imagining the women as girls and the men as boys. They were all flawless in his mind, and he decided that some of them must've been homely. He gave some gawky arms and protruding teeth that exposed wet, meaty gums when they smiled. He found it was very satisfying to make the beautiful women into unfortunate-looking girls with long, bony faces and curveless, boy-like bodies, but when he did the same with the men, it seemed a blow to his pride. Then he imagined Georgiana as a child, her brown hair thin and falling straight. Her dress was frail and light. Was she lonely? Was she neglected? He imagined her standing alone while a group of children played nearby having already declared her anathema to their games. Then, he imagined her balancing on a plank across a muddy pond until she fell and sat with the feeling of her lonesomeness intensifying with her shame.

He stood and made his way through the park which was populated with dark, dirt trails winding through large, immovable trees. Skeletal roots were bent outward in the surface of the path like fossilized, knobby limbs. It was at the bottom of the path, in an open space between a dense bower of trees, that a cultivated patch of grass extended towards an especially dark canopy. He wondered if he ought to pick some flowers growing along the tree line. He had left the store without a gift. However, he didn't stop and the thought passed into its quiet, unviolent death.

The grass was populated with bobbing bodies of varying sizes. A spectacled father tossed a colorful ball to a young boy who persisted with ungainly enthusiasm, two girls crowded together over a patch of grass, their sticklike frames jutting from their clothes, and an old man with a wooly ring of steel-gray hair absently smiled behind his sunglasses. He had never seen Georgiana outside. She always answered the door in a robe, and at her request, he always left while she was in the shower. No matter how long he stayed, dithering at the doorway, she must, he decided, wait for the sound of him leaving. It took some work to picture her in a yellow sundress. Her ivory limbs turned up to the Sun and an uncontainable smile breaching her soft, sad face. The wad of bills was dense and stuck heavily to his leg.

He reached the other side of the grass and followed a path through the dense canopy of trees. This trail dipped steeply forcing him to rely on the outer edge of his foot as gravity and friction battled with seeming randomness for a moment of sudden supremacy. Suddenly, just as he slipped, he heard some guttural yelling rebounding off the scattered boles. Then, he listened for a moment unsure whether or not it was merely the roar of the gravel beneath his feet. He caught the sound again, realizing that there were two voices: one was especially loud like a particularly vicious bark and the other was venomous and vitriolic as it hissed beneath. He followed the path and discovered that it bent towards a small enclosure where two men were standing face to face with an iron tension building in their bent limbs. One man had three men behind him and the other had five. All was grimly quiet save these two men yelling; that is until their yells stopped and every man turned upon Robert as if they would put away their current grudge to deal with the offense of his gazing. Not intended for public consumption, Robert thought and quickly continued on. He thought they had a bit of Mandy inside them, or Mandy had a bit of them especially the louder fellow. Some strain of DNA shared from the same primeval grandfather. She had the same contortion of the face and the same jutting of the jaw. If he didn't know her family, he would've guessed they were siblings. He did not feel the same license to unrestrained anger. He had never done that. He had never haphazardly released every ounce of indignation but also, he must concede, no one had ever done to him what he had done to Mandy.

The path straightened out while the trees thinned. Gradually, he saw blue pinnings of sky between the light shadow of the canopy, and then, after a moment's walking, he was out of the park and back onto the street. He had been deposited into a cobbled lane blocked off from any intruding cars. A great many shops lined these streets; many of them with a warm, welcoming glow as though lit by some Old World flame. He considered each window as he passed and decided on one not because of its contents but because a young, pretty woman caught his eye, and he decided this was a shop for young, pretty women. The shop was small, and the front window now seemed ridiculously large when viewed from within. He quickly discovered this young woman was not a patron but the sole proprietor when she offered her ever ready assistance.

"A gift," he said.

"And for what?" she asked with girlish bluntness.

"No occasion really. An apology, I suppose."

"A woman?" she smiled slightly.

He nodded.

"What does she like?"

"I'm not sure. We've only just started to get to know each other."

She smiled with spaced teeth, and the down on her cheek caught the light. "Well, what type of woman is she?"

"I don't know what to call it. She's a bit counterculture but no tattoos, no piercings but against the grain if you understand me."

"With women, I think jewelry is always safe."

"I might not be describing her well."

"Jewelry is safe," she said again with playful finality.

He trusted her and felt some emanating warmth teasing his instincts. He felt he must be doing something right by women and this woman recognized that. She led him to a wall of drawers labeled with white adhesive tape and black bunched letters only the young woman could decipher with perfect accuracy. He stood close to her finding an intimacy in their shared occupation. He thought the fabric of her pants very thin and her arms very brown. She pulled a drawer out towards them, and it dropped obediently displaying its piled contents to their crowding heads. Her gentle-looking fingers somewhat harshly sifted through thin pieces of silver. She brought up two earrings and held them up before her face, and he saw that her

neck was very slight, too slight it seemed to hold her head. He worried that he could not touch it. His brutish clumsiness seemed a constant threat to its delicate and slim bend. "What do you think of these?"

"Her ears aren't pierced."

"Really?"

"Positive." Her little lobes slightly yellowed with spiderlike hairs were one uninterrupted bulb reminiscent of the bulge of her cheek. She sifted through another drawer with one finger as though she were drawing in the sand. From the drawer, she produced two rings. One was thick with a speckled trail engraved like a band, and the other was thin and wound like two densely nutating vines.

"I think those will do," he said.

She led him to the counter where she placed the rings between mounds of velvet in a small box and covered them. He took the wad of cash from his pocket and handed her two bills.

"Keep the change."

She pushed the box forward with the tips of her fingers which he grazed when his hand jumped to palm the small cardboard box. Why, he wondered as he left, does it seem that they like us so much more when they think we are taken.

He arrived at the building and followed a familiar path up the stairs. She answered her door in her bathrobe which hung halfway down her thigh. She stood with her skin made soft and red from a recent shower. Her light brown hair was tightly bound to the back of her head with dark, damp strands interlaced in its absorbent furrows. This young woman had him step inside, and he produced the wad of cash from his pocket.

"This is forty short."

He sprung out with the small cardboard box resting in his palm. She considered it for a moment, her cheek solidly still. Then one long foot stepped forward, and she slid the box from his hand. She stood there with the box opened, her silent face with a milk-white undertone gently focused on those two silver rings. "I still need the rest."

"Of course, of course. I happened to see them is all, and well . . ." He let the final word hang in the air alongside his hands as his shoulders bunched into a shrug as though she should be fully aware of the completed utterance. She stood straight, her thin arms now crossed, and she seemed to prefer the floor to his smiling, sweaty face. "Will you come by next week with the rest?"

He agreed and seemed set to stay a while longer in his spot smiling at this young woman with her face in the carpet.

"You know, I have another appointment."

"Of course. I'll come by same time."

After he left, she sat on the edge of her bed in what she realized was the very same spot his wife had sat some weeks earlier. The young woman had answered her door and found this small woman with a curled bunch of hair and boxlike jaw considering her as though she were revolving some candied venom in her tight-lipped mouth.

"Are you Georgiana?"

"Yes," she had replied.

This small woman had stepped inside and considered her mattress and her dresser with a small porcelain ballerina in its eternal pose. "Do you know who I am?" she asked with a pointed, interrogatory quickness. After Georgiana shook her head, this woman declared she was Robert's wife. She took advantage of the younger woman's quiet, confused shock to accuse her in a calm, iron-like tone. Why had her husband visited her apartment so often? Was he buying her gifts? Taking her to dinner? Paying her suspectedly paltry rent? She then became very agitated, unwilling to break off her string of condemnatory questions. Bolstered in anger, her deep, demanding tone took on a very dreadful ire. Had the younger woman no shame? Couldn't she get her own husband or must she spend her life playing with others? Did she know that her brother was a marine? That she hated her? That she could burn down this entire building? Here, she had ended abruptly as though she had breached the pinnacle of her rage and no extant elevation could carry her higher.

The young woman then began in very timid tones to explain that she was not her husband's lover but that she was no single man's lover. The small woman fell to that spot on the bed and broke into a horrendous wracking of sobs that dominated the heavy and silent air while the young woman, her legs uncomfortably bare in her robe, could only stand idly by.

George Salis

Smog Mammoth

Gather round first-last fire ashes ugh listen. Ice fangs noses, ice shrinks eyes, ugh frosts hearts, gives kin chill skin, but ice not always on kin. Short-short time, not so long past, kin had sun-piece ugh no ice, clean noses, clear eyes, ugh full hearts, gave kin nice warm hair skin. Before first-last fire, night be dark night, night be storm night, kin sat deep in earth-shell, youngs to she-men chests, sky-cracks in ears, quaked all kin. Then kin heard sky-crack so loud. Kin thought, Earth-crack? No-fear, all-scar Karv left earth-shell ugh saw tree-crack. Karv later said, "Karv no cry," but kin knew Karv cried. Karv loved tree, hugged tree, kissed tree. Now tree-crack! Then Karv saw sun-piece in tree-crack. Blue ugh purple ugh green, but all yellow ugh red. Gold! So bright that Karv did not see for beat, beat, beat, but then Karv whacked own eyes ugh saw. Egg-shaped sun-piece. First-last fire! With lilac sky-cracks all round, Karv tried to grab sun-piece but sun-piece bit Karv hands, then Karv tried to kick sun-piece like bear skull game but sun-piece bit Karv foot. Karv later said, "Karv no cry," ugh kin knew Karv did not cry. No-fear, all-scar Karv felt no pain. But Karv felt hunger from sun-piece bite smells on Karv hands ugh foot, ugh Karv did not want to be beast-feast. Karv picked up stick that fell off tree Karv loved then Karv stabbed sun-piece ugh held sun-piece high like night-sky-sun. Night be dark night, night be storm night, but Karv be warm, ugh when Karv gave smile, Karv three teeth glowed in light.

Back in earth-shell, kin thought Karv be deep-sleeped. Kin thought sky-crack made Karv crack, soon beast-feast. Word true that no-fear, all-scar Karv be most strong, ugh she-men licked lips when she-men laid eyes on Karv meat or just whiffed Karv dirt-sweat stench, but kin has horde of strong men deep-sleep tales: like tale of strong-man Bur, who could crush skulls with own skull but one day took too long nap in earth-shell shade ugh woke in earth-shell bear cub group. Bear cubs wet-nosed Bur, play-pushed ugh play-shoved, then Bur be forced to eat goo greens that earth-shell bear ma brought to cubs, ugh Bur threw up goo greens. While new-Bur cub kin ate fresh paunch-thrown share, earth-shell bear ma sniff-sniffed man-paunch juice ugh charged Bur with bone-white fangs ugh night-black claws, ugh Bur ugh bear ma brawled with sheer earth-sky force—growl-whack ugh snarl-snap ugh roar-rip—but bear ma skull too tough ugh crushed Bur skull, ugh red man-juice sight-smell made cub kin turn into cub foes when all cubs mauled Bur till Bur be beast-feast, ugh later found with large night-sky light-hole in gray skull-brow.

While first-Karv she-man Egra let tears leak, light-point grew in night-black earth-shell mouth, from fire-fly to sun-piece torch gripped in Karv fist. Kin yipped ugh howled, kin clapped palms ugh stomped soles, ugh Egra tried to hug Karv but Karv pushed Egra down ugh held sun-piece high, near to earth-shell spike-roof. So bright that for beat, beat, beat, no one saw things, no one heard sounds, no sky-tears, no sky-cracks. Just fire-wrap ugh far-deep spike-drips. But then kin whacked own eyes ugh saw no-fear, all-scar strong-man Karv ugh Karv night twin on earth-shell wall. When Karv took steps to kin, Karv night twin took steps to kin, but Karv night twin moved like drunk snake, moved with sun-piece. Karv laid down sun-piece torch on earth-shell floor heart, ugh said, "Gift . . . gift to kin." Kin saw how sun-piece hiss-chewed on stick, ugh all kin placed sticks near sun-piece, ugh sun-piece grew to huge sun-piece, huge fire. Men, she-men, ugh youngs felt own arms ugh legs, nice warm hair skin, then kin saw earth-shell wall night kin, tall short thin fat weak strong, ugh aped night kin drunk snake moves, ugh night kin aped kin, which kin aped, which night kin aped . . . till kin danced ugh pranced with night kin round first-last fire ugh night kin danced ugh pranced with kin.

As kin danced, sky-cracks turned into sky-drums, sky-tears into sky-taps. Boom-rang one-brow Toz ugh Toz night twin blew in vulture flute ugh made twice toot sounds. First-last fire breathed out smoke to mask earth-shell roof.

She-men ugh she-men night twins threw ugh caught youngs like roly-polies ugh youngs ugh night twin youngs laugh-screeched. Beard-clothes Drul ugh Drul night twin did back flips ugh front flips, then fell near first-last fire ugh Drul flailed ugh writhed as first-last fire fizz-gulped spark-coughed all beard-clothes, ugh kin laughed ugh called Drul no-clothes, ugh no-clothes Drul rubbed black-marked chin ugh frowned with first-seen nude lips. Earth-shell mouth breathed in fog to mask earth-shell floor. Pink-eyed, see-through she-man Von spun ugh hopped ugh made Von flash-gleam twins on earth-shell wall floor roof. First-Karv she-man Egra ugh Egra night twin twirled hair like whip on Karv meat back ugh Karv smacked own chest ugh barked with she-man thirst. Second-Karv she-man Lebi ugh third-Karv she-man Unu ugh Lebi-Unu night twins joined hair-whip rite on Karv meat back chest legs. Me, bent-thumb Gurk, knifed air with Gurk arms ugh smacked Gurk knees while Gurk earth-shell wall-paints blinked ugh shook ugh squirmed. Between night twins, me saw Gurk-paint bison graze, horse rear, ibex climb, ugh earth-shell bear scratch. Me, bent-thumb Gurk, heard of earth-shell wall-paint magik, but saw first time! With joy of magik ugh first-last fire, me caught two roly-poly youngs ugh swirled one on Gurk scalp, one on Gurk tip-finger. All smiles, all laughs, then young on Gurk scalp grabbed Gurk ears ugh said, "Big mam-mam!"

Kin saw Gurk-paint mammoth lines float in air for beat, beat, beat, big, big, big, then earth-shell roof smoke ugh earth-shell floor fog mixed in Gurk-paint mammoth lines to make Smog Mammoth. As she-men gasped ugh used she-men backs to shield youngs, Smog Mammoth bellowed with beast-rage ugh charged to first-last fire ugh all jumped out of Smog Mammoth path. With Smog Mammoth trunk Smog Mammoth snatched first-last fire ugh shoved fire in beast mouth ugh coughed smoke rings, but first-last fire be not deep-sleeped. First-last fire woke in Smog Mammoth eyes! Blue ugh purple ugh green, but all yellow ugh red, red, red! All-strength, all-round Gord, who could chew big stones then poop small stones, clutched Smog

Mammoth tusks ugh tried to snap tusks like twigs, but Smog Mammoth breathed first-last fire on Gord head. While all-strength, all-round Gord screamed ugh smacked own head, Smog Mammoth stomped-burst Gord bod like grape ugh dashed to night-black earth-shell mouth. Boom-rang one-brow Toz peeled off one-brow ugh hurled one-brow at Smog Mammoth bum, but one-brow came back to Toz hand no-blood clean, ugh Toz spat on one-brow ugh pressed one-brow to brow-bone with scowl-sigh. At same time, no-fear, all-scar Karv slung spear at Smog Mammoth bum, but later found spear stuck in earth-shell wall. No-clothes Drul shook Drul man-tail ugh yelled, "Smog Mam has fear-fear!"

In wet-dark earth-shell, kin coughed ugh she-men cried. First-Gord she-man Muda said, "All-strength, all-round Gord be . . . deep-sleeped . . . cuz Gord fought for all!"

No-fear, all-scar Karv said, "Hunt-pack go make Smog Mam deep-sleep. Go now!"

First-Gord she-man Muda laughed with frown ugh said, "Karv hid with fear as all-strength, all-round Gord fought."

No-fear, all-scar Karv smacked own chest ugh said, "Karv be no fear, all scar!"

Muda wringed air with Muda hands like stick-bug, "Muda saw all-fear Karv!"

Sky-sun fed fire-light to earth-shell mouth ugh Karv stood tall in fire-light ugh touched Karv meat spots, "Snake kiss, earth-shell bear kiss ugh claw-touch, horse hoof-touch, spear-tooth—"

Muda laughed loud ugh said, "Kiss ugh touch like she-men."

First-Karv she-man Egra clomped to Muda face ugh said, "No-fear, all-scar Karv saved Muda from wooly rhino when all-round Gord got rounder on one-man beast-meat-feast."

Muda slapped Egra ugh then Muda ugh Egra brawled on earth-shell floor till boom-rang one-brow Toz grabbed Muda arm ugh Egra arm ugh pulled left-right.

Me, bent-thumb Gurk, yelled, "Stop!" All be still. "First storm nights ugh dark nights, then more storm, more dark, more cold. All be bad, all be bad-bad. Kin needs to be We, not one ugh one ugh one . . . Kin needs first-last fire to not deep-sleep in storm-storm nights ugh dark-dark nights. Kin needs first-last fire for nice warm hair skin, not wet cold chill skin.

"Long time, long-long past, when all be ice, long-long kin fought not just beasts but sky-ice ugh earth-ice ugh more. All be freezed, all be deep-sleeped. Long-long kin called it . . . ice age. Long-long past soon turn into now."

Pink-eyed, see-through she-man Von, lost in dark, be voice in kin heads, "Bent-thumb Gurk speak true-true. Kin small, kin weak. Kin needs first-last fire to live ugh grow."

She-men moms spoke as one, "Think of youngs. Kin can't warm youngs with wet cold chill skin or feed youngs with freezed breast-juice. Think of youngs!"

When Muda ugh Egra calmed, boom-rang one-brow Toz let go ugh said in coarse voice, "Be good."

No-fear, all-scar Karv growled ugh said, "Talk ugh talk, but Smog Mam run ugh run."

No-clothes Drul, clothed in dark, nodded ugh said, "Time be now!"

Kin made messy poll ugh chose no-fear, all-scar Karv with spear, no-clothes Drul with club, boom-rang one-brow Toz with boom-rang one-brow. Pink-eyed, see-through Von said, "Von be no-seen by kin, ugh not have youngs ever. Choose Von, ugh Von can save kin so kin can see Von first time." Von be born with stealth, skilled with shiv, ugh Von be known to pick fruit ugh plants in full beast sight, but kin did not choose Von. Then kin told buzz-chest Vlork, who could rub-rub Vlork palms on Vlork chest-hairs then use Vlork tip-fingers to zap-zap beasts, to stay with kin, to hunt ugh fight for kin while hunt-pack deep-sleeped Smog Mammoth.

Me, bent-thumb Gurk, be awed when kin chose Gurk too, cuz me fabler, me earth-shell wall-painter. Kin said me, bent-thumb Gurk, had to go, had to see ugh know tale to tell tale, as me do now. In own head me, bent-thumb Gurk, vowed to paint no more. If me did not paint

earth-shell wall mammoth, then no Smog Mammoth. Gurk hands be rude to earth-shell wall-paint magik. All-strength, all-round Gord deep-sleeped. First-last fire in Smog Mammoth mouth ugh eyes. Gurk fault . . .

Before Smog Mammoth hunt, first-Gord she-man Muda gave me, bent-thumb Gurk, all-strength, all-round Gord sling-shot ugh Gord small stone poop bag. "All-strength, all-round Gord loved Gurk tales. Gord fav tale be tale of strong-man Lar who picked up earth-peak to let weak kin pass ugh find more food."

Me, bent-thumb Gurk, smile-frowned. "Me now know tale of strong-man Gord, who could chew big stones then poop small stones, who could sling-shoot beast eye from far-far. All-strength, all-round Gord who fought Smog Mammoth."

Muda held tears in ugh said, "True-true."

"Quick-quick!" yelled no-fear, all-scar Karv. "No time!"

Muda looked in Gurk eyes ugh gave smile. Me gave nod ugh met hunt-pack by earth-shell mouth. Karv-Toz-Drul-Gurk hunt-pack stood in loop ugh knocked fight-arms. "Ugh, ugh, ugh!" Outside, all be cracked ugh wet from dark-dark storm. Kin huts wrecked ugh flat. Me said, "Earth-shell saved kin." No-clothes Drul walked through wreck ugh picked up deep-sleeped Drul dad gray-shrunk beard-clothes, which Drul had kept to hang above bed, but beard-clothes turned into wet-ash in Drul hands, ugh Drul made fists. Me, bent-thumb Gurk, knelt at bowl of dried Gurk-paints ugh saw haze lines, lines in shape of deep-sleeped strong-man with sky-crack through strong-man head. Magik sign? Boom-rang one-brow Toz found first-last deep-sleeped Toz she-man Snolli ibex bone neck-chain ugh held in tears ugh tied neck-chain to Toz wrist. Karv stared at fav tree, now tree-crack, then shook Karv head ugh said, "No time!" No-clothes Drul said, "Look." Char-tracks burnt into ground, huge dark discs like deep-sleeped sky-suns. No-fear, all-scar Karv squeezed spear ugh said, "Smog Mam." Boom-rang one-brow Toz rubbed boom-rang one-brow ugh said, "Hunt be cinch."

Hunt-pack ran char-track course ugh went left right right left right, no, right left left right left, or hunt-pack just jumped from deep-sleeped sky-sun to deep-sleeped sky-sun like tale of strong-man Rib who used Rib thighs to hop from base cliff to top cliff, till hunt-pack stopped at plant-thick sky-tear woods with Smog Mammoth-shape dug-burnt through. Boom-rang one-brow Toz said, "Kin does not go in sky-tear woods . . ." No-fear, all-scar Karv said, "Smog Mam go. Hunt-pack go. No fear!" Hunt-pack heard creaks ugh moans ugh shakes. No-clothes Drul, man-tail between Drul legs, said, "What first-last beasts could feast on hunt-pack in sky-tear woods?" Me, bent-thumb Gurk, told tale of strong-man Dam who went in plant-thick sky-tear woods to hunt new food for weak kin. Two days gone, Dam crawled back with much Dam skin flayed to show red-red Dam meat ugh all hair on Dam bod ripped off. Strong-man Dam yelled, "Dam no food Dam no food Dam no food," till Dam deep-sleeped same night. Karv said, "Dam one man, hunt-pack four man. Strong-man Dam not strong. Hunt-pack strong." Toz gave nod ugh said, "No-fear, all-scar Karv be right. Ugh what beasts did hunt-pack see till now? Beasts have fear-fear." Me, bent-thumb Gurk, said, "Beasts fear hunt-pack, but now be not same as past hunt-packs. Smell Smog Mammoth char-tracks," ugh all sniff-sniffed ugh hunt-pack nose-holes twitch-twitched, "Fire ugh deep-sleep. Beasts fear Smog Mammoth smell more." No-clothes Drul sneezed ugh said, "Char-track smell be black magik." Me, bent-thumb Gurk, stared at ground. Boom-rang one-brow Toz peeled off one-brow ugh held one-brow like shiv, then said, "Could Smog Mam sleep in own sky-tear-woods shell now? Cinch to deep-sleep. Half there . . . ."

Hunt-pack growled, "Ugh, ugh, ugh!" With fight-arms in fists, hunt-pack went in plant-thick sky-tear woods where Smog Mammoth dug-burnt sky-tear-woods shell. Smog air made hunt-pack cough-cough ugh put fur-clothes to hunt-pack mouths ugh nose-holes. No-clothes Drul now beard-scarf Drul, so Drul put beard-scarf to Drul mouth. Wilt-leaves fell from top.

Ground all ashes ugh squashed plants. But hunt-pack went ugh went ugh found no Smog Mammoth with shut-eyes, just more ugh more dug-burnt sky-tear woods. Hunt-pack knew no day, no night, cuz plant-thick sky-tear woods too plant-thick, too dark. Burnt green ugh gray ugh brown all round. Me, bent-thumb Gurk, coughed hard-hard ugh said, "Me have thirst." Gurk throat dry ugh itch-itch. No-fear, all-scar Karv raised fist with spear ugh said, "Stop . . . sound." Hunt-pack gathered ugh listened. Beard-scarf Drul ear twitch-twitched ugh Drul said, "Water sound. Like storm night but not." Boom-rang one-brow Toz used one-brow shiv to point straight, "Light-hole." Hunt-pack whacked own eyes ugh gave nod. For beat, beat, beat hunt-pack breathed through fur-clothes then dashed to light-hole, past singe-leave swarms ugh burnt-blooms like black sky-clouds. Crunch, crunch, crunch went ashes below hunt-pack feet. Beard-scarf Drul fell ugh made ash plume ugh hunt-pack helped beard-scarf, ash-clothes Drul up. Light-hole now light-mouth. Fight-arms gripped, hunt-pack walked through light-mouth.

So bright that for beat, beat, beat, no one saw things, no one heard sounds, no creaks, no shakes. Just green light-wrap ugh far-deep water-rush. But then hunt-pack whacked own eyes ugh saw big spring space with fresh-wet grass ugh rich blooms ugh three clean lakes, plant-thin sky-tear woods. "Oooh." Water fell above huge mid lake. Light-holes in green plant-sky. Toz rubbed face in grass ugh gave sigh. Me, bent-thumb Gurk, knelt at first lake ugh gulped. Beard-scarf, ash-clothes Drul said, "One uhhh two uhhh three!" As Karv gripped spear in Karv hands ugh growled, "Stop," Drul ran-howled to second lake ugh jumped to make ball-bod splash. Then second lake stilled. Karv asked, "Drul?" For beat, beat, beat, second lake stayed still, but then frothed ugh out came Drul feet, legs, ugh man-tail. Hunt-pack laughed at beard-scarf Drul head-stand ugh leg split. Then hunt-pack heard moan-yawn-creak ugh man-trap plant jaws rose from fresh-wet grass lake-rim ugh closed on second-lake mouth. "Drul!" Me, bent-thumb Gurk, pulled back Gurk head to dodge man-trap plant jaws that closed on first-lake mouth. As second-lake man-trap plant stalk grew into green plant-sky, hunt-pack heard hushed Drul water-yells in man-trap plant head. Me put poop stone in sling-shot sling ugh slung-shot poop stone that punched hole into second-lake man-trap plant which made bright green water leak. At same time, no-fear, all-scar Karv slung spear ugh pierced man-trap plant to make bright green water leak from second hole. But man-trap plant still lived, still made Drul beast-feast. Boom-rang one-brow Toz tossed one-brow ugh one-brow arced ugh sliced man-trap plant stalk ugh man-trap plant head fell on fresh-wet grass ugh burst like grape ugh beard-scarf Drul washed up at hunt-pack feet, all still ugh stained with bright green, ugh Toz caught one-brow ugh spat on one-brow ugh pressed one-brow to brow-bone with smile, then Karv spear washed up too.

Karv knelt by Drul ugh smacked Drul back ugh Drul cough-coughed bright green water, then Drul eyes grew big-big ugh Drul rolled in fresh-wet grass ugh yelled, "Drul no food Drul no food Drul no food." Hunt-pack be shocked that such blue lake water could turn into bright green plant-paunch juice that stung ugh burned. Plant-feast! To clean plant-paunch juice from Drul skin, hunt-pack took out man-tails ugh peed on Drul skin. Drul showed Drul five teeth ugh spread mouth wide-wide ugh smacked own cheeks ugh neck ugh screamed, "Save Drul!" So hunt-pack peed in Drul mouth. Beard-scarf, pee-clothes Drul gargled hunt-pack pee ugh spat then drank more ugh gulped hunt-pack pee to clean deep-deep in paunch. Karv laugh-laughed ugh asked, "Drul good now?" Drul groaned ugh put Drul hand to own paunch ugh said, "Drul has paunch-ache . . . all lakes fake . . . all man-trap plants!"

Hunt-pack heard loud-loud moan-yawn-creak like sky-crack, like earth-crack, ugh huge man-trap plant jaws rose from fresh-wet grass mid-lake-rim ugh huge man-trap plant stalk reared. As huge man-trap plant water-roared, no-fear, all-scar Karv cried, "Deep-sleep man-trap plant!" "Ugh, ugh, ugh!" Man-trap plant vines whipped out of plant water-throat ugh snared hunt-pack necks ugh arms ugh legs. Fight-arms fell. Hunt-pack tried to move but plant vines choked-choked ugh cut-cut, then plant vines flipped hunt-pack on backs, dragged hunt-pack near ugh near ugh near. Beard-scarf, pee-clothes Drul groaned with paunch-ache-ache, Karv yelled with rage, boom-rang one-brow Toz used Toz bottom lip to blow on one-brow to get one-brow from brow-bone but could not, ugh me, bent-thumb Gurk, thought of hunt-pack paint ugh man-trap plant paint on future earth-shell wall, Karv-Toz-Drul-Gurk hunt-pack deep-sleeped but alive in kin-tales . . . Then me, bent-thumb Gurk, saw flash-gleam shiv ugh one by one man-trap plant vines snapped ugh hunt-pack be freed. Pink-eyed, see-through Von! Toz-Drul-Gurk yipped ugh howled as hunt-pack got fight-arms. Von said, "Like with kin, Von be no-seen by hunt-pack. Can hunt-pack see Von now?" Karv made no sound till Karv said, "Pfft! Hunt-pack must deep-sleep man-trap now!" Man-trap plant water-roared ugh spewed bright green paunch-juice from water-throat, but hunt-pack jumped out of paunch-juice fall-path. Pink-eyed, see-through Von said, "Nuh-uh! All kin be deep-sleeped if hunt-pack be deep-sleeped. Hunt-pack must live, must hunt Smog Mam now." Toz-Drul-Gurk said Von spoke true-true. No-fear, all-scar Karv scowl-scowled. More vines, like full hair, whipped from man-trap plant water-throat ugh grasped at air all round. "Von knows way!" Von held shiv high like first-last fire ugh, as hunt-pack trailed shiv flash-gleams, hunt-pack stabbed ugh sliced ugh clubbed ugh slung-shot man-trap plant vines, till hunt pack ran deep into new dug-burnt Smog Mammoth-shaped hole, safe-safe in thick-plant sky-tear woods.

With rage, no-fear, all-scar Karv stomped to pink-eyed, see-through Von face ugh yelled, "Man-trap plant deep-sleeped strong-man Dam ugh near deep-sleeped hunt-pack. Karv should deep-sleep man-trap plant!" Von shiv flash-gleamed on Karv throat ugh Von said, "Want big-big scar, Karv?" Karv skin turned all red but Karv stood still for beat, beat, beat, then took step back. Von pink-eyes glow-glowed, "Karv does not care for strong-man Dam. Karv just cares for Karv tales. Hunt-pack needs to hunt Smog Mam. Karv get big Karv tale then." Karv growled ugh clomped to light-hole ugh hunt-pack went too. Me, bent-thumb Gurk, said, "Von saved hunt-pack. Hunt-pack thanks Von." Drul ugh Toz said, "Thank-thank, Von!" Ugh hunt-pack saw Von pink-back, strong ugh scarred. Through more singe-leave swarms ugh burnt-blooms like black sky-clouds, hunt-pack jogged. Crunch, crunch, crunch went ashes below hunt-pack feet. Boom-rang one-brow Toz said, "Light-hole be . . . odd." Hunt-pack stared at light-hole, ugh light-hole turned black ugh purple ugh white ugh black again. Flash-flash. Beard-scarf, pee-clothes Drul said, "Light-hole lives?" Me, bent-thumb Gurk, said, "Like fire-fly." Crunch, crunch, crunch, flash, flash, flash, till hunt-pack heard booms like storm-storm night. When light-hole turned into light-mouth, hunt-pack saw huge gray plain ugh gray sky, then all white, then plain ugh sky, then all blue, then plain ugh sky. Boom-boom, boom-boom-boom, boom. Blue ugh purple ugh lilac sky-cracks all round, one ugh two ugh five ugh eight ugh more than Karv bum hairs! Drul, with Drul hands on Drul ears, said, "Sky-cracks, but no sky-tears." Karv stared into air ugh said, "Sky not sad. Sky just mad." Von gave nod ugh said, "Mad-mad." Me, bent-thumb Gurk, held Gurk palm out of Smog Mammoth-shaped hole-mouth ugh caught sky-ice flake, "Ice age." Sky-crack light made Karv-Toz-Drul-Gurk see Von bod-lines, Von strong-scar breasts ugh strong-scar back ugh strong-scar bum, all scar like all-scar Karv ugh no clothes like no-clothes Drul, then dark made Karv-Toz-Drul-Gurk no-see Von, then sky-crack light again . . . With eyes on ground, Von said, "No char-track . . . but Smog Mam smell tells Von that Smog Mam charged through sky-crack plain ugh into earth-peaks." Hunt-pack saw far earth-peaks half hid in earth-ice ugh hunt-pack skin shook with cold.

Sky-crack struck near Smog Mammoth-shaped hole-mouth ugh hunt-pack ears crack-cracked ugh hunt-pack eyes did not see for beat, beat, beat, beat, beat, beat. Beard-scarf, pee-clothes Drul, with Drul thumbs deep in Drul ears, yelled, "Does just one sky-crack deep-sleep man? Two sky-cracks? Three?" Me, bent-thumb Gurk, with Gurk hands on Gurk ears, yelled tale of strong-man Lit who be struck by sky-crack ugh kin thought Lit be deep-sleeped. As kin dug earth-bed for deep-sleeped strong-man Lit, Lit woke ugh sky-crack tats on Lit skin glowed yellow ugh purple. After, for earth-shell hunts ugh night hunts, Lit be light for kin in dark. But Lit sleeped no nights, cuz Lit saw sky-crack flash-flash in shut-eyes. Lit eye-crack. Ugh Lit heard sky-crack boom-boom in Lit ears, more loud than Lit heart. Lit ear-crack. Kin said one day, after days ugh days of no sleep, while on Lit-lit night hunt, Lit turned into pure sky-crack ugh shot into black sky-cloud paunch for deep-deep-sleep. Kin said sky-crack booms be Lit snores.

No-fear, all-scar Karv banged spear bum on ash ground ugh said, "Sky-cracks deep-sleeped Karv fav tree ugh deep-sleeped strong-man Lit. Karv deep-sleep sky-cracks!" Karv flexed Karv meat ugh charged into gray sky-crack plain with spear held high like first-last fire—

"Karv!" called hunt-pack—then spear glowed like first-last fire, then Karv bod glowed too. With lilac sky-cracks all round, Karv be sky-cracked ugh lay deep-sleeped.

Boom-rang one-brow Toz said, "Karv be . . . deep-sleeped?" Pink-eyed, see-through Von said, "Karv be dumb-dumb. Keep fight-arms down. Walk slow-slow ugh keep hunt-pack eyes out." Hunt-pack crept through gray sky-crack plain. With sky-crack-cracks came flash-flash ugh flash-flash, which made hunt-pack look like hunt-pack paint on white-air wall, on blue-air wall, on purple-air wall. Paint then not paint, paint then not paint, so fast that flash-flash dazed hunt-pack. But pink-eyed, see-through Von pink-eyes ugh strong-scar back glowed bright-bright ugh Von led Toz-Drul-Gurk between, above, below blue-purple-white-lilac sky-cracks like thick plants ugh vines. Flash-flash ugh flash-flash. Hairs on hunt-pack heads stood like sky-sun spikes ugh bod hairs stood like grass. Boom-boom-boom-boom-boom. Sky-ice fell like slow sky-tears. Fizz-sting, fizz-sting, fizz-sting went gray plain below hunt-pack feet till hunt-pack reached no-fear, all-scar, deep-sleeped Karv. Boom-boom, boom-boom-boom, boom. Karv mouth be gaped, Karv eyes be shut, ugh Karv skin glowed ugh thawed sky-ice dust. Boom-rang one-brow Toz touched Karv brow but Karv brow zapped Toz tip-finger like buzz-chest Vlork, "Ow!" Hunt-pack stared between Karv eye-brows at fresh sky-crack tat. Boom-boom-boom-boom, boom-boom-boom, boom. Me, bent-thumb Gurk, said, "Sky-crack tat be . . . tree-shaped." Pink-eyed, see-through Von said, "Quick-quick," ugh put deep-sleeped Karv on Von strong-scar back then picked up seared Karv spear. Flash-flash ugh flash-flash ugh boom-boom ugh boom-boom. To help, me, bent-thumb Gurk, held Karv left leg on Gurk shoulder ugh beard-scarf, pee-clothes Drul held Karv right leg on Drul shoulder, ugh hunt-pack crept through gray sky-crack plain. Flash-flash made hunt-pack turn hunt-pack paint on white-air wall, on blue-air wall, on purple-air wall. *BOOM!* Bright-bright black ugh dark-dark white all round.

At dawn, Von-Drul-Gurk hunt-pack woke in earth-peaks with Karv face ugh Toz face above, Karv-Toz breaths like small sky-clouds. Sky-ice fell more thick than gray sky-crack plain sky-ice. No-fear, all-scar Karv said, "Rest." Karv tree-shaped sky-crack tat be dim blue. Drul said, "Drul be . . . deep-sleeped?" Karv-Toz laughed ugh Toz said, "Just sleeped." Von said, "Huh?" Toz said, "As hunt-pack held deep-sleeped Karv high, Karv be struck by sky-crack again, through Karv meat back to Karv meat heart." Karv said, "Uh-huh! Sky-crack woke Karv, sleeped Von-Drul-Gurk. Karv saved Von-Drul-Gurk on Karv meat back." Toz said, "Von on Toz back." Karv slapped Toz head ugh said, "Toz lies. Karv saved all. Toz too ty-ty to walk so Karv picked up Toz too. True-true, Toz?" Toz one-brow made V above Toz eyes ugh Toz growled. Me, bent-thumb Gurk, said, "Thank-thank." Drul said, "Thank-thank." Karv said, "Nuh-uh. Thank-thank hunt-pack. Hunt-pack We, hunt-pack One." Von said, "Hunt-pack be four ugh one when dumb-dumb Karv ran into gray sky-crack plain." Karv turned red ugh sky-crack tat

flashed, but Karv just said, "Hunt-pack rest." Von-Drul-Gurk skin felt fizz-stung, zap-zapped. Pink-eyed, see-through Von stared at earth-peaks ugh earth-peaks, lots, all hid by ice, mixed with white-white sky. Von said in soft voice, "Half see-through." To make good mood, beard-shirt Drul used Drul fizz-pricked lips to play vulture flute, short toot sounds. Boom-rang one-brow Toz spread Toz arms ugh fell back in earth-ice with smile, then swished Toz arms to make Toz earth-ice twin with wings, bird-Toz. Me, bent-thumb Gurk, wiped sky-ice from Gurk arms ugh breathed small sky-cloud into Gurk hands ugh rub-rubbed. Once Drul vulture flute song be done, all be quiet for long-short time, just sky-ice wind-moans, till Karv paunch growled like earth-shell bear ugh Karv said, "Karv starve-starve." Toz said, "Karv-Toz hunt. Von-Drul-Gurk rest."

Karv-Toz flexed Karv-Toz meat, "Ugh, ugh ugh," held spear ugh boom-rang-one-brow high like first-last fire, then trailed beast-smells into far sky-ice white. Von-Drul-Gurk lay with Von-Drul-Gurk bods close ugh napped. Me, bent-thumb Gurk, dreamed of sky-sun turned sky-rock, deep-sleeped, ugh all be sky-ice, earth-ice, kin-ice, hut-ice, beast-ice, but Gurk skin burned with hot ugh me yelled, "Gurk no food Gurk no food Gurk no food." Ugh then, all be sky-fire, earth-fire, kin-fire, hut-fire, beast-fire, but Gurk skin shook with cold ugh me said, "Gurk no live Gurk no live Gurk no live." When me, bent-thumb Gurk, woke, Karv-Toz hunt-pack came back with deep-sleeped bone-wing deer on Karv-Toz back. Karv-Toz hunt-pack dropped bone-wing deer by Von-Drul-Gurk. Drul rubbed Drul eyes with fists. Von yawned ugh swiped at sky-ice like flies. Bone-wing deer jaw be loose from Toz boom-rang one-brow slice, ugh bone-wing deer neck red-mouthed from Karv spear stab. Pink-eyed, see-through Von sat up ugh said, "Hard-hard hunt?" No-fear, all-scar Karv said, "No-hard hunt! Cinch!" Von used Von strong-scar hand to pet deep-sleeped bone-wing deer fur, ugh said, "Von could hunt bone-wing deer with no-blood, just no-seen shiv-hole between bone-wings." Karv frowned ugh used teeth-blade to cut up hunt-catch, Karv hands fast but with shake.

Later, as hunt-pack chew-gnawed bone-wing deer meat, me, bent-thumb Gurk, told tale of bone-wing deer. "Long time, long-long past, bone-wing deer had no bone-wings on head, but bird-wings on back. Beasts charged bird-wing deer for beast-feast, but bird-wing deer flew high-high ugh beasts starve. So beasts asked laugh-sneak jackals to help, ugh one night, when bird-wing deer dreamed of full life in sky, jackals held laugh in ugh moved bird-wings from deer back to deer head. But next day when beasts charged bird-wing deer for beast-feast, bird-wing deer still flew high with bird-wings on head. So beasts asked black-magik snakes to help, ugh one night, when bird-wing deer dreamed of earth with no beasts, snakes used black-magik night-eyes to stare-stare ugh turn bird-wings on deer head to bone-wings. Ugh next day, when beasts charged bone-wing deer for beast-feast, bone-wing deer could not fly high-high or low-low, just run-run with bone-wing weight on head, then beasts had bone-wing deer feasts."

Beard-shirt Drul said with full Drul mouth, "Hunt-pack be beasts."

Pink-eyed, see-through Von gulped ugh said, "Karv-Toz-Drul-Gurk be beasts."

No-fear, all-scar Karv belched loud like sky-crack boom ugh said, "Von beast too."

Von pink-eyes flashed as red-eyes.

Me, bent-thumb Gurk, said, "Bone-wing deer does not fly, but bone-wing deer knows now to fight with bone-wings."

Boom-rang one-brow Toz wiped bone-wing deer meat-blood on Toz arm ugh said, "True-true. Karv near got new scar." Karv threw bone at Toz head but Toz dodged ugh said, "Toz saved Karv from Karv chest scar."

Karv bit own fist then said, "Toz all-fear, no-scar!"

Beard-shirt Drul laughed. "Toz-Gurk-Drul saw Von. Did Karv see Von? Karv bod be just scarred, but Von bod be scar-scarred."

Karv-Toz-Gurk-Drul stared at Von bod, see-through, but with stare-stare Karv-Toz-Gurk-Drul saw pink lines ugh holes, all scar. Von looked down at bone-wing deer scraps.

Me said, "Like earth-shell wall-paints."

Karv took big-big bite of bone-wing deer meat ugh chomped with blood scowl.

With sad Toz eyes, cuz Von no-fear had made Toz think ugh think of first-last deep-sleeped Toz she-man Snolli, Toz said, "Why Von be all scar?"

Just sounds of chew-gnaw-chomp ugh sky-ice wind-moans, then Von said, "Cuz when kin no-sees Von, Von likes to see beasts ugh sleep near beasts."

Karv spat bone ugh said, "Von fights beasts?"

Von used Von nail to pick Von teeth, then looked at Von nail, "Uh-uh. But times when Von sleeps too close to beasts. Beasts no-see Von, but beasts feel Von ugh strike at Von air."

Karv raised Karv fists. "Then Von fights beasts!"

"Uh-uh."

Drul wiped blood from Drul mouth to beard-shirt. "What Von do?"

"Von runs ugh runs . . . goes back to be no-seen by kin."

Toz stroked boom-rang one-brow ugh said, "Von should learn beast-talk. In tale of she-man Sog, Sog knew beast-talk ugh made beasts kin."

Me, bent-thumb Gurk, smeared blood from hands to earth-ice. "But when Sog met spear-tooth cat ugh asked, 'Spear-tooth be kin?' spear-tooth cat made Sog beast-feast."

Toz hiccupped. "Beast-feast?"

"Cuz spear-tooth be bad man-talk. Spear-tooth true-true name be no-known roar."

Karv smacked own chest ugh gave smile with Karv three teeth. "Von can be fourth-Karv she-man." Karv stared at Von strong-scar breasts ugh licked Karv blood lips. "Good-good she-man. Karv can warm Von."

Beard-shirt Drul gave hoot ugh tugged on Drul man-tail.

Von held up shiv ugh tapped shiv point with Von tip-finger. "Von be not cold, not hot, not warm. Von be no-seen, so Karv soon have no-seen shiv hole on Karv head-top."

Karv laughed like bear-jackal. "Von cold-cold!"

Me, bent-thumb Gurk, said, "Von speaks true-true."

Karv raised white-white bone ugh snapped bone in half, "Shut Gurk mouth . . . or Karv shut Gurk."

Toz stood, stretched ugh smacked Toz thighs, ugh said, "All hunt-pack had rest. Time to hunt Smog Mam."

For beat, Karv sky-crack tat flashed like sky-sun third eye. "Hunt-pack waste-waste-waste time! Toz said Von nose good-good, but if Von nose no good, Karv bite Von nose off!"

Paunch-filled, hunt-pack hiked through earth-ice up to hunt-pack ankles, pink-eyed, see-through Von in lead. Wind-ice pecked hunt-pack faces ugh hands. Wind-moans filled hunt-pack ears with vague tales of deep-sleep, but me, bent-thumb Gurk, be not in tale-mood. Over wind-moans, hunt-pack heard far roar-roar. Boom-rang one-brow Toz looked into white-white ugh said, "Smog Mam?" Von said, "Uh-uh." Von strong-scar nose twitch-twitched, sniff-sniffed, but after long-short hike-time Von looked lost. No-fear, all-scar Karv said, "Von nose good Karv bum!" Von wiped sky-ice from nose-holes, then Von nose twitch-twitch-twitched, sniff-sniff-sniffed ugh Von said, "Beast be near . . ."

Hunt-pack heard growl-growl like rock slide. Out from white-white stalked spear-tooth cat king, big as five spear-tooth cats, with spear-teeth long as Smog Mammoth tusks ugh flash-gleam sharp. Spear-tooth cat king eyes be dark-dark like gray sky-rock ugh spear-tooth paunch be pulled in with starve-starve. Spear-tooth breath rose from spear-tooth nose-holes like gray sky-clouds, like first-last fire smoke.

All stood still, till Karv raised spear high like first-last fire ugh said, "Deep-sleep spear-tooth!"

Spear-tooth cat king head went low-low ugh spear-tooth back sloped up, primed to pounce on hunt-pack. Karv threw spear, Toz tossed boom-rang one-brow, ugh me, bent-thumb Gurk, slung-shot poop stone. Boom-rang one-brow nicked spear-teeth, poop stone broke on spear-tooth ear, ugh spear-tooth cat king dodged Karv spear ugh bit spear mid-air ugh spear snapped in half like bone. "Ugh, ugh, ugh!" Drul charged with club held high like first-last fire but slid on earth-ice into black-snot pit.

Spear-tooth cat king pounced at Karv-Toz-Gurk, but Karv-Toz-Gurk dodged spear-tooth cat king ugh Von stepped near with Von arms spread wide ugh high. Spear-tooth cat king eye-eyed Von bod-lines through spear-tooth breath-smoke then saw flash-gleam when Von dropped shiv in earth-ice. Beard-shirt, black-snot pants Drul yelled, "Save Drul, save Drul!" Karv-Toz-Gurk stood still, eyes on pink-eyed, see-through Von, till Von breathed deep ugh tried true-true beast-talk spear-tooth name with roar like spear-tooth cat king, like sky-crack boom across all earth-peaks, across all earth. Hunt-packed looked at tensed spear-tooth cat king. "Save Drul!" But spear-tooth cat king gave small growls like laugh then raised huge spear-tooth paw with spear-tooth claws ugh slashed Von down.

With Toz hand stretched out, Toz cried, "Von!"

Karv said in voice draped in sky-ice wind-moans, "Von no-no fear, all-all scar . . ."

Karv-Toz-Gurk saw Von bod lined with Von blood, not see-through, but bright red, red-red, red-red-red!

Toz thought of first-last deep-sleeped Toz she-man Snolli, who, when Toz left with hunt-pack, fought off jackal-pack to save youngs, but claw wounds on Snolli bod made Snolli deep-sleep after two days of ill-ill ache-pain with Toz at Snolli side. Toz smelled Snolli claw wounds like murk worms, heard Snolli snarls like starve-thirst beast, ugh saw Snolli eyes like wild wake-dream.

Toz gave war-cry, pain-cry. Me, bent-thumb Gurk, be cold as sky-ice ugh earth-ice, with white-white Gurk skin, ugh Gurk eyes saw all as earth-shell wall-paints, true but not true. Karv made tight-tight fists, so tight that Karv blood leaked through Karv fingers. Karv sky-crack tat glowed bright-bright blue-purple-white-lilac ugh Karv clomped to spear-tooth cat king with Karv meat flexed, "Spear-tooth? HA! Twig-tooth! Twig-tooth with fear-fear!"

"Save Drul, save Drul!"

With beast-rage, spear-tooth cat king roared true-true name, so loud-loud that Karv-Toz-Gurk fell to Karv-Toz-Gurk knees, stunned, ugh spear-tooth cat king opened spear-tooth mouth wide to make Karv beast-feast, but Karv shook-shook ugh shook-shook, ugh Karv thought of time when Karv be young ugh lost from kin for days ugh had starve-starve till fruit fell on young Karv head-top ugh young Karv had fruit-feast then gave tree hug ugh kiss . . . Then Karv scream-screamed ugh shot blue-purple-white-lilac sky-crack beam out of tree-shaped sky-crack tat ugh spear-tooth cat king had sky-crack beam-feast ugh spear-tooth paunch grew-grew, then sky-crack tats spread across spear-tooth fur, blue-purple-white-lilac, bright, bright, bright, till spear-tooth cat king bod grew-grew-grew big as earth-peak ugh *BOOM!*, then fell sky-tears of spear-tooth cat king meat ugh blood ugh bone. "Save Drul, save Drul, savbspdrsbsp-drbs—" As spear-tooth cat king chunks roar-fell past Toz-Gurk ears, Toz-Gurk gained sense ugh saw Karv fall to earth-ice in pain-pain. Me went to Karv while Toz went to Von. Sky-crack beam had burned off all Karv clothes. Sky-crack tat on Karv meat back had spread black ugh white, made hole that showed Karv spine ugh Karv heart. Beat, beat, beat, beat-beat-beat! Me said, "Wh-what, wh-wh—" Karv swung Karv arm to shoo Gurk ugh yelled, "Go! Deep-sleep Smog Mam! Karv fine. Sky-crack force gave strength, take strength." "Me just fabler, just earth-shell wall-pa—" "Help-help Von. Hunt-pack not just Gurk, not just Karv. Hunt-pack We, hunt-pack One. GO!" In beat, beat, beat, beat-beat-beat, Karv meat fizzed ugh melted like earth-ice ugh Karv turned into bone Karv. Me, bent-thumb Gurk, whacked own eyes but Gurk eyes saw

true-true. No-fear, all-scar Karv be deep-sleeped.

At same time, boom-rang one-brow Toz thought Von be deep-sleeped ugh cried till Toz saw Von breaths that made small-small sky-clouds, so Toz quick-quick patched spear-tooth cat king claw wounds on Von face-chest-thighs with magik tree sap kept in pouch.

Me, bent-thumb Gurk, thought, Where be Drul? Me looked ugh looked then saw just Drul arms that poked out of black-snot pit ugh Drul black-snot air bubbles. Me grabbed Karv thigh bone ugh ran to help Drul. Drul palm felt Karv thigh bone ugh grabbed tight, ugh me pull-pulled ugh pull-pulled till Drul head came slow-slow up from black-snot pit. Drul head be black-snot drenched ugh Drul nose sneezed black-snot mist. Me pull-pulled ugh pull-pulled till Drul chest came slow-slow up, then Drul man-tail, then Drul legs, then Drul feet. Black-snot-clothes Drul sneezed ugh sneezed ugh coughed black-snot plume.

Me said, "Drul?"

Drul hawked black-snot ball, made black-snot fart bubbles, then said, "Thank-thank-thank-thank Gurk!"

Me, bent-thumb Gurk, pinched Gurk nose with Gurk bent-thumb ugh point-finger. "Do not thank-thank Gurk. Thank-thank Karv."

Drul looked at Karv thigh bone in Gurk hand, then past Gurk at Karv bod bones. "Karv be . . . deep-sleeped."

Me, bent-thumb Gurk, gave nod.

While Drul cried black-snot tears, Drul used Drul tip-finger to shut nose-hole one then from nose-hole two blew black-snot slug. "Karv fought with sky-crack strength."

After black-snot-clothes Drul roll-rolled in earth-ice, then tied long-long beard round Drul bod, now beard-clothes Drul, like before first-last fire fizz-gulped spark-coughed all Drul beard-clothes, hunt-pack gathered round Karv bones, weak-weak pink-eyed, see-through Von on Toz back. Me, bent-thumb Gurk, said, "Tale of strong-man Karv be done," ugh thought, If me did not paint earth-shell wall mammoth, then no Smog

Mammoth. All-strength, all-round Gord be deep-sleeped. No-fear, all-scar Karv is deep-sleeped. Gurk fault . . . With flash-gleam tears, Von said, "Karv be dumb-dumb." Toz knelt ugh slow-slow put Von down, ugh said, "Karv dreamed to be Karv fight-arm when deep-sleeped." All quiet for long-short time, just sky-ice wind-moans, as Toz turned Karv bones into Karv spine-spear. When done, ugh after hunt-pack dug earth-bed for rest of Karv bones, Toz held Karv spine-spear high like first-last fire, ugh yelled, "Ugh, ugh, ugh!" As Toz pump-pumped Karv spine-spear in air, all hunt-pack yelled, "Ugh, ugh, ugh! Ugh, ugh, ugh! Ugh, ugh, ugh!"

When Von be on Toz back again, beard-clothes Drul wiped black-snot from nose-holes ugh said, "Like Karv say, 'Deep-sleep Smog Mam now!'"

With chill skin, hunt-pack hiked through earth-ice up to hunt-pack shins, ugh though pink-eyed, see-through Von be weak-weak, Von sniff-sniffed ugh used Von teeth to tug on Toz right ear ugh Toz left ear to show way. Wind-moans filled hunt-pack ears with clear tales of deep-sleep ugh me, bent-thumb Gurk, saw deep-sleeped strong-men as earth-shell wall-paints on white-white all round. Strong-men Bur, Karv, Lar, Gord, Rib, Dam, Lit, ugh more, all strong, all deep-sleeped . . . Me whacked own eyes ugh blink-blinked then saw just white-white, till sky cleared small bit ugh hunt-pack saw more than white. Hunt-pack be on earth-ice plain between earth-peaks, with herd of freezed ground sloths all round. Beard-clothes Drul wiped black-snot from nose-holes ugh said, "Sloth skin be chill-chill." Boom-rang one-brow Toz gave nod ugh said, "Ice-ice." Most ground sloths be freezed in thick ice-rocks like bugs in sap. All ground sloths had sad-scared ground sloth faces. Von spoke in soft voice, "Soon hunt-pack ugh kin be ice-ice too . . ." Me, bent-thumb Gurk, said, "If hunt-pack does not deep-sleep Smog Mammoth . . ." Hunt-pack hiked past more ugh more freezed ground sloths, like blue-white woods, then Von nose sniff-sniffed ugh twitch-twitched ugh said, "Von smells rage ugh starve-starve. One sloth be not freezed . . ."

Between rows of freezed ground sloths, earth-ice cracked ugh crunched as not-freezed ground sloth charged at hunt-pack ugh yelled, "Men iced kin! Gwûg full-doze men!"

With Von on Toz back, Toz hid behind freezed ground sloth in ice-rock. Von said, "Put Von down."

Toz said, "Uh-uh."

"Von can fight!"

Toz shook Toz head ugh said, "Von be weak-weak. Von dumb-dumb too?"

Von bit Toz ear till Toz ear bled but Toz did not move.

At same time, me, bent-thumb Gurk, crouched ugh saw beard-clothes Drul sneeze black-snot mist which made ground sloth Gwûg stomp back in shock, then Drul charged with club held high like first-last fire, but when Drul swung club Gwûg stood on Gwûg hind legs, more tall than two strong-men stacked, ugh dodged club ugh club crushed freezed ground sloth. With sad-mad Gwûg face, Gwûg yelled, "Coz Mörg!" Gwûg raised ground sloth claws like shiv-fingers ugh said, "Man . . . man full-dozed Gwûg coz Mörg. Gwûg full-doze man!" But Drul held club high like first-last fire, set to crush second freezed ground sloth. "Back beast! Or Drul crush-crush more sloth kin."

"Not gam-gam Hæg!" Gwûg brown eyes turned red-red ugh Gwûg let out low growl. Gwûg claws scraped ugh scraped earth-ice, soon to strike Drul down in rage, but me, bent-thumb Gurk, held Gurk hands up, walked to Gwûg, ugh said, "Wait-wait!"

Gwûg red-red eyes stared into Gurk eyes. Me said, "Men did not freeze ground sloths. Men can't make sky-ice, just as men can't make sky-sun or earth-peaks or sky-clouds. Like long-long past, now be . . . ice-age."

Gwûg eyes turned dull red ugh Gwûg claws stopped earth-ice scrape ugh scrape. "Ice age? How?"

Drul held club low.

Me said, "Men do not know, beasts do not know. But hunt-pack fight ice age ugh Gwûg can help hunt-pack, help ground sloth kin too."

Gwûg eyes turned brown, then back to dull red. "This be man trick?"

"Uh-uh."

Beard-shirt Drul said, "Gurk . . . no time. Beast can't trust hunt-pack, hunt-pack can't trust beast." Ugh Drul held club high like first-last fire again, then Gwûg growl-growled.

With Gurk palms up ugh out, me yelled, "Wait-wait-wait-wait!"

When Drul-Gwûg calmed, me, bent-thumb Gurk, said, "With no trust, all ground sloths ugh men soon be deep-sleeped. Short-short time, not so long past, men kin had sun-piece ugh no ice, clean nose, clear eyes, ugh full heart, gave kin nice warm hair skin."

Gwûg head cocked to one side, "Gurk mean blaze-heart?"

Gurk finger aimed at sky-sun, "Gwûg saw sun-piece? First-last fire?"

Gwûg claw aimed at place in blue-white woods with no freezed sloths, just long black-black marks like Smog Mammoth char-tracks. "Black-air Mam with blaze-heart eh blaze-eyes came through plain eh breathed blaze on . . . Gwûg iced kin. Gwûg charged Black-air Mam but Black-air Mam left fast-fast past earth-peak. Gwûg stayed to guard rest of Gwûg iced kin."

With Von on Toz back, Toz came from behind freezed ground sloth in ice-rock ugh held Karv spine-spear high like first-last fire ugh said, "Hunt-pack hunts for Smog Mam. First-last fire can help men kin ugh sloth kin."

Gwûg eyed Karv spine-spear, eyed Toz-Gurk-Drul, then whacked Gwûg paws twice on Gwûg chest. "Men hunt-pack strength with Gwûg strength can full-doze Black-air Mam."

Hunt-pack yelled, "Ugh, ugh, ugh!"

Gwûg yelled, "Eh, eh, eh!"

Then pink-eyed, see-through Von said, "Like Karv say, 'No time!'"

Gwûg head cocked to left side, "Man with man head eh haze-haze she-man head?"

Hunt-pack laughed ugh boom-rang one-brow Toz turned to show Von full bod on Toz back.

Gwûg head cocked to right side, "Ah. She-man can't walk? She-man slow hunt-pack down."

Von pink-eyes glowed. "Von can walk."

Beard-shirt Drul said, "Von be weak-weak from great beast-fight."

"Nuh-uh. Von can walk." Von used Von teeth to tug on Toz ear. "Put Von down."

"But Von be weak-we-ow!" Toz one-brow made V above Toz eyes ugh Toz growled.

Von said, "Want Von to have Toz ear-feast?"

Gurk-Drul laughed ugh Toz put Von down, but when Von tried to walk Von legs bent ugh Von fell in earth-ice with cry-moan.

Toz tried to help Von up but Von smacked at Toz to shoo Toz.

Gwûg mouth gave pout. "Slow-slow hunt-pack down . . ."

Me, bent-thumb Gurk, said, "Von fights best. Von can get well, then hunt-pack be strong-strong."

Toz growled at Von then said, "Like Von said Karv say, 'No time!'" Von scowled ugh looked off at earth-peaks while Toz put Von on Toz back.

With chill skin, hunt-pack hiked through earth-ice up to hunt-pack knees for long-long time, past freezed bison, freezed horses, freezed ibex, freezed jackals, freezed spear-tooth cats, freezed earth-shell bears, freezed bone-wing deer, ugh more, till, half-up once far-far earth-peak, night came ugh hunt-pack had rest in freezed woods, blue-white like freezed ground sloths. No need to hunt, so hunt-pack sat in loop ugh had freezed beast-feast ugh Gwûg had freezed grass-feast, all mouths crunch-crunched, all tongues too chill to taste.

Night sky flash-gleamed with chill-chill wind-ice, ugh me, bent-thumb Gurk, spied half-blue light-holes.

While Gwûg big jaw chewed, Gwûg said, "What does Gurk see?"

Me said, with Gurk finger aimed at night sky, "Light-hole spear . . . light-hole hunter . . . light-hole sky-shell bear king."

Boom-rang one-brow Toz breathed Toz breath on freezed spear-tooth cat leg to make spear-tooth cat leg thaw small bit, then said, "Do light-holes make shapes for sloths?"

Gwûg said, with Gwûg claw aimed at night sky, "Light-drip tree trunk . . . light-drip ground sloth paw with one claw . . . light-drip claw-tooth king."

Beard-clothes Drul gave smile, blood ugh meat crumbs in Drul teeth. "Claw-tooth king? True-true! Man sees light-hole spear-tooth cat king. Same-same."

Gwûg head bowed small bit. "Eh night-cliff, what men see in night-cliff?"

Me said, "Night-cliff . . . sky-rock?" Gwûg gave slow nod ugh blink. Me said, "Sky-rock has man face with scars, so sky-rock must be hunter, fighter."

Pink-eyed, see-through Von shut one Von pink-eye ugh used Von thumb ugh point-finger to pinch sky-rock. "Sky-rock be she-man paunch, paunch filled with youngs."

Gwûg said, "Hmm . . . one time, night-cliff be climbed by ground sloth king Nön, eh Nön told sloth kin other side of night-cliff be second sky-blaze. Blaze-cliff!"

Me held out Gurk palm, "Sky-sun," then flipped Gurk palm down, "Ugh second sky-rock?"

Gwûg stopped grass-chew ugh eye-eyed Gurk bod ugh said, "Gurk does not look like hunter. Gurk has much more know-know than scars."

Drul said, "Bent-thumb Gurk bent Gurk thumb on first-last hunt ugh—"

Me said, "First-last hunt till now . . . On first hunt, odd, small sky-rock-piece fell from sky, ugh all dodged but Gurk. Me had raised Gurk hand to . . . block sky-rock-piece? Catch sky-rock-piece? Gurk does not know. But sky-rock-piece struck ugh broke Gurk thumb. After days, Gurk broke-thumb cured into bent-thumb. Later, buzz-chest Vlork found same-same odd, small sky-rock-piece in bush, all black-black ugh hole-filled, ugh gave sky-rock-piece to Gurk as joke."

"Hmm . . . why Gurk on Black-air Mam hunt now?"

Von, with scar-scars that flash-gleamed like half-blue light-holes, said, "Gurk be man kin fabler, ugh good with sling-shot."

Gwûg head cocked to one side, "Fabler?"

Toz spat spear-tooth cat bone piece ugh said, "Gurk knows ugh tells all kin tales ugh beast tales."

"Hmm . . . Gurk knows ground sloth tales?"

Me said, "Uh-huh." Hunt-pack ugh Gwûg gathered round freezed spear-tooth cat bones ugh listened. "Ground sloth used to be small-small ugh slow-slow, but when ground sloth saw mammoth, ground sloth craved to be big-big ugh not as slow-slow. So, one day, ground sloth ma snuck ground sloth young into mammoth water-hole, ugh mammoth drank ugh sucked young up mammoth snout ugh gulped young down. Inside, ground sloth young crawled from mammoth paunch to womb, as ground sloth ma had told ground sloth young to do. Later, ground sloth young be twice-born as big-big ugh not slow-slow ground sloth, like Gwûg."

While me, bent-thumb Gurk, had told tale, Gwûg had held in laugh, Gwûg paws on Gwûg paunch. Now Gwûg laugh-laughed slow-deep ugh said, "Bison poop! Ground sloth kin always big-big ugh strong-strong, not small-small ugh slow-slow. Don't Gurk know? Other way round. Young mam crawled into ground sloth womb to grow big-big," ugh Gwûg laughed more.

Hunt-pack gave smile, but when Von said, "Gurk be earth-shell wall-painter too," me, bent-thumb Gurk, frowned ugh looked at light-hole mammoth in night sky.

"Hmm . . . hmm . . . Gwûg has seen earth-shell wall-marks left by men. Gwûg likes earth-shell wall-marks. What has Gurk made?"

Wind-ice moans snaked through freezed trees all round. Me, bent-thumb Gurk, looked at night-night between light-hole mammoth light-holes, ugh said, "When buzz-chest Vlork gave black-black sky-rock-piece to Gurk, me stroked ugh rubbed sky-rock-piece, ugh sky-rock-piece made Gurk hands black-black. Me stare-stared at Gurk hands, Gurk palm-lines, ugh me felt need to go into earth-shell ugh use Gurk bent-thumb to paint on earth-shell wall . . . Me made many paints with sky-rock-piece, like Gurk-paint horse, ibex, earth-shell bear, but first Gurk-paint be mammoth . . . now Smog Mammoth."

Gwûg head cocked to left side, then to right side, "Black-air Mam?"

Pink-eyed, see-through Von said, "Not Gurk fault . . ."

Me said, "Gurk fault! If me did not paint earth-shell wall mammoth, then no Smog Mammoth. All-strength, all-round Gord be deep-sleeped. No-fear, all-scar Karv be deep-sleeped. Gurk fault . . ." Me shook-shook not just from chill skin but from rage ugh shame.

Von shook Von head ugh said, "Nuh-uh. Not Gurk fault."

Me gave sigh ugh made small-big sky-clouds. "Gurk hands be rude to earth-shell wall-paint magik."

"Hmm . . . night-cliff magik."

Von put Von strong-scar hand on Gurk back. "Gurk tells tales ugh makes paints, brings earth-sky-beast force to life-life. Not rude."

"Hmm . . . night-cliff chose Gurk."

Me thought, If sky-rock, night-cliff, chose Gurk . . . why? Me looked at dark earth-ice with haze of small sky-rock twin for beat, beat, beat, then Gurk hands made fists, "Me, bent-thumb Gurk, vowed to paint no more."

Beard-clothes Drul wiped black-snot from nose-holes ugh said, "Drul has seen . . . Gurk not weak-weak." Drul smacked own chest. "Do not be weak-weak inside. Gurk must fight, must turn weak inside into strong outside."

Boom-rang one-brow Toz said, "True-true. Like how Toz turned big-long one-brow into boom-rang after youngs laugh-laughed at Toz . . ." Toz licked Toz tip-finger ugh wiped Toz tip-finger across Toz one-brow, which flash-gleamed with ice-bits. "Toz hears no laughs now."

Drul said, "Gurk must turn tales ugh paint into fight-arms. Like Toz, like Von see-through skin stealth."

Me looked at hunt-pack faces, Drul ugh Von ugh Toz ugh Gwûg, then said, "Like tale of strong-man Karv, who loved trees since Karv young, but Karv tree-love made youngs laugh-laugh too, so one day young Karv snuck-tailed hunt-pack to show strength ugh when hunt-pack fought earth-shell lion-pack, young Karv dashed from bush ugh used sharp stick to stab-stab earth-shell lion neck ugh save hunt-pack head. Young Karv got first, but not last, scar. Later, when sky-crack deep-sleeped tree that Karv love-loved, Karv fought many sky-cracks till sky-crack deep-sleeped Karv, but Karv woke with sky-crack force in Karv bod, ugh later used sky-crack force to deep-sleep spear-tooth cat king."

"Hmm . . . Karv strong-strong man."

Hunt-pack said, "True-true!"

Me, bent-thumb Gurk, gave smile small bit.

Gwûg said, "All rest now, eh then hunt-pack can hunt under blaze-cliff."

Thick-thick wind-ice blew with wind-howls. While ice-bits flash-gleamed on hunt-pack bods, hunt-pack breathed small sky-clouds into hunt-pack hands ugh rub-rubbed.

Gwûg said, "Gwûg fur more thick-thick than iced air," ugh Gwûg lay on Gwûg side ugh spread Gwûg long arms, but hunt-pack eyes stared ugh hunt-pack skin shook-shook. "Come. If hunt-pack be full-dozed, then all will be full-doze. With ice-age, all be kin, all be One." Ugh hunt-pack pressed into Gwûg chest ugh Gwûg long arms wrapped hunt-pack like fur-fur earth-shell.

Under sky-sun, blaze-cliff, hunt-pack woke with nice warm hair skin, till Gwûg yawn-yawned slow-deep ugh spread Gwûg long arms, then hunt-pack skin turned chill-chill with wind-ice.

Gwûg said, "Morn! Good doze?"

Hunt-pack said, "Uh-huh. Thank-thank Gwûg."

Cuz of magik tree sap, spear-tooth cat king claw wounds on Von face-chest-thighs turned into thin scars quick-quick. Pink-eyed, see-through Von stood ugh when Von tried to walk Von legs moved well. "Does hunt-pack see Von? Von can walk!"

Boom-rang one-brow Toz held in tears.

Gwûg gave slow blink ugh said, "Gooooood. Von can make hunt-pack more strong."

Hunt-pack yelled, "Ugh, ugh, ugh, eh, eh, eh!"

Toz held Karv spine-spear high like first-last fire, then held Karv spine-spear out to Von. "Toz heard . . . Karv said, 'Von no-no fear ugh all-all scar.'"

Slow-slow, Von took Karv spine-spear. "Hunt-pack can *see* Von . . ." Pink, see-through tear trailed from Von pink-eye. "Thank-thank Toz."

Toz shook Toz head. "Do not thank-thank Toz. Thank-thank Karv."

Von gave nod then held Karv spine-spear high like first-last fire.

Hunt-pack yelled, "Ugh, ugh, ugh, eh, eh, eh!"

With chill skin, hunt-pack hiked through earth-ice up to hunt-pack thighs, Gwûg in lead to move much earth-ice with big-big Gwûg bod ugh Gwûg long arms ugh Gwûg claws. Hunt-pack saw sky-clouds turn into huge ice-rocks, bird-flocks freezed like blue-white spear-heads. As sky-ice all round shrunk sky-sun, hunt-pack got chill-chill skin ugh whacked own bod to break off ice. After long-long time, more than half-way up earth-peak, Gwûg stopped ugh eye-eyed earth-peak tip-top.

Me, bent-thumb Gurk, said, "What Gwûg see?"

Gwûg said, "Hmm . . ."

Toz said, "Like second small-small sky-sun."

Gwûg nose ugh Von nose sniff-sniffed ugh twitch-twitched.

"Black-air Mam."

Von gave nod ugh ice broke off Von neck.

Hunt-pack said, "Deep-sleep Smog Mam!"

With chill-chill skin, hunt-pack hike-hiked through earth-ice as Gwûg moved much-much earth-ice till far Smog Mammoth be not-so-far Smog Mammoth, perched on earth-peak tip-top. Hunt-pack heard Smog Mammoth smoke-moans ugh fog-groans, then Smog Mammoth head turned to look at hunt-pack with first-last fire Smog Mammoth eyes. Blue ugh purple ugh green, but all yellow ugh red, red, red! More bright than near-deep-sleeped sky-sun.

Toz freezed one-brow made V above Toz eyes ugh ice broke off Toz one-brow ugh Toz yelled, "Give first-last fire back!"

Smog Mammoth bellowed with beast-rage ugh breathed long fire which thawed much earth-ice between hunt-pack ugh Smog Mammoth, spread of mist ugh water.

Von held Karv spine-spear high like first-last fire, then pulled Von strong-scar arm back, set to throw, but Smog Mammoth stomp-smashed earth-ice with big-big Smog Mammoth legs ugh breathed more first-last fire which made earth-peak earth-ice shake-shake-fall-fall. Like water-way, hunt-pack slid with earth-ice down earth-peak, nuh-uh, up earth-peak, or hunt-pack just flew through freezed sky with ice-ice up to hunt-pack chests, hunt-pack necks. Me, bent-thumb Gurk, between chill-chill coughs, screamed like young. Pink-eyed, see-through Von be quiet ugh used Von strong-scar arms to stay above earth-ice fall. Gwûg long arms stuck out but then Gwûg sunk-sunk. Boom-rang one-brow Toz tried to swim but Toz bod roll-rolled, thrashed with earth-ice. Beard-clothes Drul be nude now, Drul long beard not tied ugh Drul beard moved ugh curved like long fur snake over earth-ice fall, ugh Drul yelled, "Grab Drul beard! Grab Drul beard!" Me, bent-thumb Gurk, reached for Drul beard tip as Drul beard snaked over earth-ice fall, but Drul beard curved to Von ugh Von strong-scar hand grabbed Drul beard. Von yelled, "Grab Drul beard!" With Von strong-scar arms ugh legs, ugh Drul beard in grip, Von swam up earth-ice fall, nuh-huh, down earth-ice rise, ugh grabbed Gurk hand then me grabbed Drul long beard. Me, bent-thumb Gurk, could not see Gwûg, but Toz head popped up from earth-ice fall ugh me yelled, "Grab Drul beard!" Von swam-swam near Toz ugh Toz coughed up earth-ice then grabbed Drul long beard. Drul yelled, "Earth-peak cliff!" Hunt-pack saw all earth-ice fall over earth-peak cliff ugh me saw big-big Gwûg bod roll over too. "Gwûg!" As Von-Gurk-Toz went over cliff with much-much earth-ice, Drul dug Drul feet into earth-peak rock ugh stood-stopped at earth-peak cliff-edge. Von-Gurk-Toz gripped Drul long beard tight-tight ugh earth-peak earth-ice turned into thick-freezed sky-tears that whack-smacked Von-Gurk-Toz heads. With Drul hands on Drul thighs, Drul stood in squat like over earth-hole to poop ugh bellowed with rage-strength, Drul jaw pulled open by Von-Gurk-Toz weight. Ugh earth-ice still fell over cliff, split in two falls by Drul squat-bod. As earth-ice roared past Drul ears, Drul used all meat strength to stay still. At same time, Drul could hear in Drul head deep-sleeped Drul dad Har, "True-true men have long-strong beards." Drul jaw bone strained ugh creaked with Von-Gurk-Toz weight. Drul thought of big-thick Har fingers that poked young Drul chin. Har laughed like mam trunk snorts ugh said, "Fruit fuzz! True-true men need no clothes, just long-strong beard ugh club."

Me, bent-thumb Gurk, had grip that near-slipped on wet Drul beard part that smelled like Drul pee. Thick-freezed sky-tears turned less thick. Toz cross-eyed, Toz spied freezed fleas between Drul beard hairs. Pink-eyed, see-through Von, gripped at Drul beard tip, yelled up to Toz, "Toz be close! Toz climb, all climb!"

Drul bod meat shook-shook not just from chill-chill but ty-ty. As Von-Gurk-Toz slow-climbed Drul beard, Drul jaw bone creak-creaked, then *CRACK!* In Drul head, Har said, "Long-strong beard good to whip she-men backs ugh bums." Drul shrieked with ache-ache-pain-pain ugh used Drul hand to feel that Drul jaw bone be broke at left hinge. Von-Gurk-Toz had slid small bit ugh near-slipped as Drul beard swung to right side, then to left side. With fear, me, bent-thumb Gurk, looked across freezed air for huge Gurk-paint bird turned into Smog Bird, with hope for paint magik to save hunt-pack from over cliff-edge.

In Drul head, Har said, "Long-strong beard good to choke ugh kill foes." Drul gripped own beard to hold Drul beard still ugh make weight light small bit. Drul yelled to Von-Gurk-Toz, "Cwimb quoyck-quoyck!"

As Toz quick-climbed Drul beard with freezed Toz hands, crazed with fear-fear, Toz thought Von be first-last deep-sleeped Toz she-man Snolli, ugh said, "Quick-climb, Snolli! Do not fall! Toz loves Snolli!"

In Drul head, Har said, "Long-strong beard good to wipe poo from own bum ugh good to floss out meat ugh bones from between teeth. But do not wipe-floss with same beard part, like Drul unk Nurv!"

In Von head, below hid fear, Von asked, Does Toz see Von at all?

In Drul head, Har said, "Long-strong beard good to hide blades ugh make dull blades sharp on coarse beard hairs."

Drul shrieked with ache-ache-pain-pain again while Von-Gurk-Toz climbed over earth-peak cliff-edge ugh when hunt-pack be saved Drul threw up earth-ice ugh blood then fell on Drul back, Drul eyes shut.

Pink-eyed, see-through Von let out sob ugh ice broke off Von lips.

In Drul head, Har said, "No Har young has fruit fuzz. True-true Har young has long-strong beard out of womb, like young Har!"

Boom-rang one-brow Toz knelt by Drul bod ugh said, "Toz can see small-small sky-cloud breaths . . . Drul be not deep-sleeped."

Von heard sound like far ice-crack ugh ice-crack. "Huh?" At last beat, before Smog Mammoth made earth-ice fall, Von had put Karv spine-spear on Von back, now Von grabbed Karv spine-spear from Von back ugh walked near earth-peak cliff-edge.

Quick-quick but with care, me, bent-thumb Gurk, ugh Toz gathered strewn Drul long beard ugh clothed Drul warm ugh tight, then Toz ripped small part of Toz clothes ugh wrapped Drul from Drul chin to head-top like when young has bad-bad tooth-ache.

At same time, in Drul head, Drul be pushed from Drul ma womb with long-strong beard round Drul neck, then Har held young Drul up from beard-noose ugh gave brown-tooth smile. Drul quick-woke with chill-chill coughs ugh freezed tears on Drul cheeks.

Drul said, "Dwuw be . . . dep-swep?" When Drul spoke, Drul jaw hinge clacked.

Gurk-Toz shook Gurk-Toz head.

Drul eyes looked at Gurk ugh Toz ugh Von. "Whay Gwû?"

Toz said, "Huh?"

Me, bent-thumb Gurk, said, "Gwûg be . . . full-dozed. Me saw Gwûg . . . Gwûg fell."

Drul eyes slow-closed for beat, beat, beat, then Drul eyes slow-opened.

Again, sound like ice-crack ugh ice-crack, more loud ugh loud. Hunt-pack eyes turned to earth-peak cliff.

Von nose sniff-sniffed ugh twitch-twitched. "Gwûg?"

Hunt-pack saw Gwûg claws grip cliff-edge— "Gwûg!"—then Gwûg long arms pulled Gwûg bod up over cliff-edge. Gwûg gave sigh ugh made big-big sky-cloud, then gave smile ugh said, "Hunt-pack!" Gwûg saw Drul on Drul back ugh said, "Drul hurt?"

Me said, "Drul saved Von-Toz-Gurk . . . with Drul long beard!"

Drul said, "Dwuw did noy siv aw hoy-poyck."

Slow-slow, Gwûg walked to Drul with Gwûg long arms out ugh gave Drul hug, then Von-Gurk-Toz joined in hunt-pack hug. For beat, beat, beat, all had not chill-chill skin, but nice warm hair skin.

Then pink-eyed, see-through Von said, "No time! First-last fire be near. Von can smell . . ."

Toz felt Toz wrist ugh Toz heart sunk . . . Snolli ibex bone neck-chain be lost. Toz held in tears ugh eye-eyed Von. Von be not Snolli, but Toz loved Von too.

Von held Karv spine-spear high like first-last fire, then used fight-arm to point at far-far huge freezed lake near earth-peak base. Hunt-pack eyes made squints ugh hunt-pack saw through

freezed air second small-small sky-sun, Smog Mammoth, on freezed lake heart, like Smog Mam taunt.

Toz said, "Smog Mam plays games."

Me, bent-thumb Gurk, said, "Long way down earth-peak . . ."

Gwûg leaned ugh used Gwûg claws to tap Gwûg big back. Gwûg looked at Gurk ugh said, "Gwûg fast-fast, not slow-slow like men eh mams. Gwûg can take hunt-pack down to full-doze Black-air Mam." Gwûg gave smile ugh said, "Quick-quick!"

Gwûg used Gwûg long arms to slow-lift Drul ugh put Drul on Gwûg big back, near Gwûg neck. Then Von climbed up behind Drul, then Toz behind Von, then me, bent-thumb Gurk, behind Toz. Like tale of strong-man Bom who jumped on horse back cuz of bet ugh rode horse for one week. Bom did not break own neck like strong-man Shrat, did not get chucked over cliff like strong-man Wik, did not have skull crushed by horse hoof like strong-man Krag, but when Bom tried to jump off horse back after week-long ride, Bom legs be stuck to horse sides with sweat-grime glue. No water or spear-pry could get Bom legs free, so Bom turned into horse-legs Bom, ugh one day, when horse-legs Bom deep-sleeped from no-known ill, Bom horse-legs be free ugh rode with deep-sleeped Bom to join horse kin again. Bom kin said that, months later, kin saw horse with vulture ugh Bom bones on back, Bom skull on horse head-top, Bom heart in vulture beak.

Hunt-pack yelled, "Ugh, ugh, ugh, eh, eh, eh!" ugh earth-peaks made same sounds.

With Drul-Von-Toz-Gurk on Gwûg big back, Gwûg used Gwûg shins ugh long arms to slide down earth-peak ugh dodge rocks ugh trees ugh freezed beasts. Drul-Von-Toz-Gurk laughed with thrill as Gwûg got air from earth-peak bumps. Ugh then, more than half-way down earth-peak, freezed sky-tears fell, big ugh small ice-rocks, some shaped like earth-shell roof spikes! While Gwûg tried to dodge ice-rocks, Drul used club to smash near-near ice-rocks. Me, bent-thumb Gurk, cheered. Toz played vulture flute with fast-fast sounds like war-cries. Von head down, Von pressed Von strong-scar bod into Toz back.

Then Drul struck round ice-rock so hard-hard—"Boye-boye, oyce-wock!"—that ice-rock flew high-high, crashed into far freezed sky-cloud, then freezed sky-cloud fell from sky ugh burst into ice-shards on far earth-peak. Hunt-pack yipped ugh howled. When small ice-rock spike grazed Drul ear ugh Drul blood fell as small-small red ice-rocks, Drul shrieked with clack-jaw ugh hit ice-rocks so hard-hard ugh quick-quick that ice-rocks turned into ice-mist.

Close to earth-peak base, sky-tear ice-rocks stopped. Once Gwûg could slide no more, hunt-pack got off Gwûg big back. With ice-fanged noses, ice-shrunk eyes, ice-frosted hearts, ugh chill skin, hunt-pack stood side to side, fight-arms held high like first-last fire, ugh marched till hunt-pack stood at freezed lake-edge.

Boom-rang one-brow Toz said, "Freezed lake freeze-freezed?"

Gwûg said, "Hmm . . . freezed lake can hold Black-air Mam."

Far Smog Mammoth be not-so-far Smog Mammoth, still on freezed lake heart, ugh hunt-pack saw how black-black Smog Mammoth skin moved like caught wind.

Me, bent-thumb Gurk, said, "But Black-air Mam be black-air ugh first-last fire. Smog. Not blood ugh bone."

As pink-eyed, see through Von used Karv spine-spear to poke lake-ice, beard-clothes Drul shook Drul head ugh said, "Dwuw be cuwsed wif bwoyck moygick. Dwuw faw thwough . . . ."

Gwûg eye-eyed Smog Mammoth blaze-eyes, ugh in first-last fire Gwûg could see rows ugh rows of iced kin, then all iced kin turned into mist, deep-deep-sleeped. Smog Mammoth blaze-eyes eye-eyed Gwûg eyes ugh Smog Mammoth bellowed with beast-rage then breathed first-last fire up into freezed air, plume of blue ugh purple ugh green, but all yellow ugh red, red, red! With tears freezed on Gwûg cheeks, Gwûg brown eyes turned red-red ugh Gwûg let out low growl ugh Gwûg claws scraped ugh scraped earth-ice.

Drul-Von-Toz-Gurk said, "Gwûg?"

But Gwûg did not hear, could not hear, cuz with rage Gwûg ran across freezed lake, ugh lake-ice crunch-crunched beneath Gwûg big bod ugh some lake-ice spots cracked small bit, like spider-webs. Gwûg yelled, "Black-air Mam made kin melt! Gwûg full-doze Black-air Mam!"

Smog Mammoth smoke-moans ugh fog-groans mixed to make smog-roar as Smog Mammoth ugh Gwûg clashed on freezed lake heart. Gwûg clutched Smog Mammoth tusks ugh tried to snap tusks like twigs, like tale of all-strength, all-round strong-man Gord, but Smog Mammoth breathed first-last fire on Gwûg chest, but Gwûg fur too thick-thick for fire to fizz-gulp spark-cough Gwûg bod like Gord head, like Drul beard, so Gwûg claws slashed Smog Mammoth throat, but just soot flew across freezed air.

At same time, beard-shirt Drul tapped Drul boot toe on lake-ice, then smacked whole Drul boot, then after Drul gave sigh, Drul jumped on freezed lake, "Ugh!" Drul gave nod ugh Drul jaw clacked. "Fweze-fwezed," then Drul looked at Gwûg-Smog Mammoth brawl—growl-whack ugh snarl-snap ugh roar-rip—ugh Drul said, "Dep-swep Smoyg Moym!"

Drul-Von-Toz-Gurk yelled, "Ugh, ugh, ugh!" ugh Drul-Von-Toz-Gurk breath made plumes of small-big sky-clouds. Life-clouds! With fight-arms raised high like first-last fire, Drul-Von-Toz-Gurk ran across freezed lake. Boom-rang one-brow Toz tossed boom-rang one-brow, ugh me, bent-thumb Gurk, slung-shot poop stone. Boom-rang one-brow sliced through Smog Mammoth head-top ugh poop stone punched through Smog Mammoth paunch, but just soot-soot flew across freezed air. Fight-arms did not hurt Smog Mammoth!

Smog Mammoth swung Smog Mammoth tusk ugh whacked Gwûg across lake-ice. Von yelled loud-loud to get Smog Mammoth blaze-eyes on Von. Like deep-sleeped no-fear, all-scar strong-man Karv, Von said, "Smog Mam? HA! Fart Mam! Fart Mam with big bum!" As Smog Mammoth charged at Von, Drul clubbed Smog Mammoth knee ugh soot puffed out like plant bloom ugh made Drul black-black beard-clothes Drul, but Smog Mammoth smog-roared ugh still charged at Von. Von leaned back with Karv spine-spear, set to stab Smog Mammoth chest, but Toz yelled, "Von!" ugh again Toz tossed boom-rang one-brow ugh boom-rang one-brow arced through freezed air ugh sliced Smog Mammoth right tusk in half. Smog-roar! No blood, but less Smog Mammoth, cuz Smog Mammoth tusk fell on lake-ice!

While me, bent-thumb Gurk, slung-shot many poop stones that punched through Smog Mammoth paunch-head-bum, like light-holes for beat, beat, beat, Gwûg picked up Smog Mammoth tusk to use as fight-arm. Gwûg eye-eyed Smog Mammoth blaze-eyes, ugh saw kin not iced but with nice warm fur, then Gwûg aimed to stab blaze-heart with Smog Mammoth tusk, but Smog Mammoth breathed much-much first-last fire on lake-ice beneath Gwûg paws ugh Gwûg fell through lake-ice into chill-chill water. Drul-Von-Toz-Gurk yelled, "Gwûg!"

Then, like on earth-peak tip-top, Smog Mammoth stomp-smashed lake-ice with big-big Smog Mammoth legs ugh breathed more first-last fire which made lake-ice melt-split-break, so hunt-pack slid-ran across web-cracked lake-ice to earth-ice before hunt-pack could fall into chill-chill water. With huff-huffs that made big-small sky-clouds, me, bent-thumb Gurk, said, "Where . . . be . . . Drul?"

Hunt-pack looked back ugh saw black-black beard-clothes Drul stuck on lake-ice piece that broke off. Drul spun round to find place to run, but all lake-ice be broke-broke. Melt-melt! With clack-jaw, Drul yelled, "Siv Dwuw, siv Dwuw!" Boom-rang one-brow Toz said, "Jump, Drul! Jump on lake-ice pieces! Quick-quick!" So Drul whacked own thighs ugh shins to break off ice, gulped Drul fear like bone stuck in mouth, then jumped from lake-ice piece to lake-ice piece like tale of strong-man Rib who used Rib thighs to hop from base cliff to top cliff. On last lake-ice piece, Drul jumped far-far . . . into Von strong-scar arms. "Phew!" Von looked at Drul, Drul looked at Von, Von looked at Toz, Toz looked at Von, Drul looked at Toz, Von looked back at Drul, then Von strong-scar arms dropped Drul on earth-ice. "Ow!"

As Drul hand rub-rubbed Drul bum, Drul said, "Gwû . . . fuw-doyze?"

Smog Mammoth stood on water like lake-ice or earth-ice ugh Smog Mammoth blaze-eyes spied hunt-pack.

Von nose sniff-sniffed ugh twitch-twitched ugh Von eye-eyed far splash-splash in water. "Gwûg!" Gwûg swam with Gwûg long arms—"Quick-quick, Gwûg!"—ugh Gwûg swam-swam ugh swam-swam, but then Gwûg crawled out of water onto earth-ice slow, slow-slow, slow-slow-slow, till, with Gwûg long arm stretched out to hunt-pack, Gwûg turned into freezed Gwûg, iced ground sloth with white fur ugh blue eyes.

Hunt-pack squeezed fight-arms tight-tight. Again, Smog Mammoth bellowed with beast-rage then breathed first-last fire up into freezed air. Tears freezed on hunt-pack cheeks, hunt-pack howled, then yelled, "Eh, eh, eh! Eh, eh, eh!"

Out of no-where, hunt-pack held in breath as sky-sun turned black, black-black, black-black-black. Night-cliff side of sky-sun? Night-feast? Sky-sun now one char-track in freezed half-night sky. Stomped on by Smog Mammoth? Not just ice age, but dark age!

Me, bent-thumb Gurk, looked round ugh saw white be black, black be white, from earth-peaks to own hands, all turned into lines, like earth-shell wall-paints. Magik! Up be down ugh down up? Right be left ugh left right?

Pink-eyed, see-through Von be not pink-eyed, not see-through, but green-eyed ugh *seen*. Black-black beard-clothes Drul be white-white beard-clothes Drul. Hunt-pack let go of breath ugh made black big-small sky-clouds.

Green-eyed, seen Von said, "Sky-sun be . . . deep-sleeped?"

White-white Smog Mammoth charged hunt-pack ugh used Smog Mammoth one-tusk to whack Toz-Drul-Von across earth-ice.

In sound of hunt-pack ugh kin voices mixed, deep-black sky-sun spoke low-low in Gurk ears, "Paint, paint, paint." With no black-black sky-rock-piece from sky, no Gurk-paints in bowl, me, bent-thumb, Gurk, knew what to do. "Paint, paint, paint. Bring earth-sky-beast force to life-life." Me whacked own chest to break off ice then used ice shard to cut-cut Gurk arm till Gurk blood flow-flowed—"Paint, paint, paint. Be not weak-weak inside."—then me, bent-thumb Gurk, sunk Gurk bent-thumb in Gurk blood, then moved Gurk bent-thumb in air, up-down, up-down, up-down, left-right, left-right, left-right—"Gurk must fight, must turn weak inside into strong outside"—till Smog Mammoth be caught in blood-paint trap for beat, beat, beat, but Smog Mammoth seeped through blood-paint trap like water through holes, then Smog Mammoth breathed first-last fire on Gurk, big stream of orange ugh yellow ugh red, but all purple ugh green, green, green! But first-last fire did not gulp-fizz cough-spark Gurk bod cuz Gurk, at last beat, had made blood-paint shield.

While Smog Mammoth coughed white smoke rings from too much first-last fire, me, bent-thumb Gurk, moved Gurk bent-thumb up, over, round, down, across black freezed air ugh made . . . blood-paint mammoth!

With not just sheer earth-sky force, but with sheer sky-sun ugh sky-rock force, Blood Mammoth ugh Smog Mammoth brawled. Growl-growl-whack! Snarl-snarl-snap! Roar-roar-rip! Blood fell like sky-tears ugh white soot spun like wind-ice.

Cuz of low-low blood, me, bent-thumb Gurk, be see-through. Me fell to earth-ice ugh, with weak-weak Gurk eyes, saw lines of Toz face ugh Drul face. "Gurk be arm-scar, bent-thumb Gurk." "Goywk hoys noy feaw-feaw."

Then Von felt hunt-pack eyes ugh kin eyes ugh beasts eyes on Von as, gripped tight-tight, Von held Karv spine-spear high like first-last fire, then pulled Von strong-scar arm back, aimed at smog-blood storm-storm blaze-heart. When Von fast-moved Von arm, flicked Von wrist, let open Von hand grip, Karv spine-spear grew wings made of sky-crack ugh flew through black freezed air, then pierced deep into Smog Mammoth blaze-heart, ugh Smog Mammoth burst-burst into soot ugh sparks. No more smog-blood storm-storm. All be still-still.

At same time, sky-sun woke from black-black-black deep-sleep.

Egg-shaped sun-piece sat in ashes ugh earth-ice stained with Gurk blood. Blue ugh purple ugh green, but all yellow ugh red. Gold!

Blood Mammoth turned into Gurk blood-pool then slid across earth-ice like snake ugh into Gurk arm wound. In awe, Toz patched Gurk ice shard arm wound with magik tree sap, then Toz ugh Drul helped Gurk up.

Hunt-pack gathered round first-last fire ugh put hunt-pack hands out ugh rub-rubbed hunt-pack hands ugh arms to get nice warm hair skin. Tears did not freeze on hunt-pack cheeks but leaked ugh dripped like water.

As me, arm-scar, bent-thumb Gurk gave smile ugh said, "Ice age no more," ashes beneath first-last fire shook, shook-shook, shook-shook-shook, till smoke seeped through ugh turned into smoke stalk with first-last fire on smoke stalk-top. Hunt-pack tried to grab first-last fire but first-last fire bit hunt-pack hands ugh smoke stalk grew into freezed sky, up, up, up, up-up-up! More tall than hunt-pack eyes could see! First-last fire shrunk . . . small, small-small, small-small-small, till first-last fire turned into new half-blue light-hole in gray sky. With fear-fear, with awe-awe, hunt-pack eyed light-hole ugh me saw that new light-hole be on tip of light-drip ground sloth paw with one claw.

Toz-Drul-Von looked down at just first-last fire ashes. But me, arm-scar, bent-thumb Gurk, eye-eyed new light-hole ugh thought, Each light-hole be first-last fire? Each first-last fire be grabbed from kin long past, long-long past, robbed by Smog Beasts to let kin freeze? Or do other men, other beasts, other no-knowns, fly-live far-far in night sky, warmed by own first-last fire?

Me, arm-scar, bent-thumb Gurk, be old-old, but you be young-young. Listen to Gurk . . . one day, kin must hunt smoke stalk in far-far night sky, must learn to live in night sky ugh be warmed by first-last fire. Or soon all kin be deep-sleeped on ice-age earth.

Shya Scanlon

Authorial Intent

P aul's young writer friend took the call. "Hi Mom. No I haven't. Sorry but I mean I'm not going to lie or circumvent the protocol or whatever. Yes I realize this affects your plans to come visit but what do you want me to do? Okay, okay, yes, I *do* know what you want me to do but like I said I—Look Mom I'm—I hope you see the irony in accusing me of being selfish. No I'm actually upstate having a socially distanced drink in the real physical world with Paul. He's that. Yes, he taught at—Yes we're—It's ridonkulous. I saw a—" Here he gave Paul a look Paul could only describe as astonished. "I'm spazzing out. What's the singular of deer."

"Deer," said Paul.

"Doesn't sound right."

"Think doe, a deer."

"Mom I saw *uh* deer. Yes I'm wearing one. I don't know I'll ask. Paul have you . . ."

Paul raised his index finger.

"So I guess he had the first one but he's fat. Mom I'm being rude. Okay I'll tell him. I love you too. Yes of course. You'll be the first to know I promise. Yes. No. Bye. Jesus. My mom says Hi. Where was I?"

"Domestic abuse."

"Right, right. You're not fat by the way, don't get a complex. What's your fauxmorbidity anyway?"

"I legitimately have high blood pressure."

"How high? Kidding. So I'm flipping through this issue of *Harper's* and there's a short story called 'Domestic Abuse' written by, do you know _____ at _____ University? And of course because of the title and because he's written autofiction since before it was a thing and I'm like this should be interesting, and it turns out that it's about, wait, you said you have or haven't read it?"

"Have not."

"It's about this guy who lands a massive, open-handed slap on his wife's face after she accuses him of fucking his student, who's staying with them at the time and so she sees this whole thing and freaks out and it's partly about does the student report him even though the wife begs her not to. Sort of a spin on *Who's Afraid of Virginia Woolf?* I mean I haven't seen it but anyway so I call the author who's an old friend of mine and I just say, *Whoa*, and he knows of course what I'm talking about. He says I wasn't the first person to call. But the point is, do you want another round? The point is that he goes on to talk about the genesis of the story."

"Is he married?"

"Yes. Gorgeous woman—can I say Black?—who does some kind of computer thing. He tells me that he'd had this idea that he wanted to write about a man slapping his wife but he didn't think he could do it because everyone knew his fiction was his life, as in if something occurred in his stories you could pretty much bet it actually happened, or something like it happened, and so everyone would automatically assume that he'd hit his wife."

"Which he hadn't."

"Well that's where it gets interesting, because I guess over the span of a month or so he begins to obsess about the idea that he isn't able to write this thing he wants to write, and though part of him knows that he put himself in this position by mining his private life for material he still feels hemmed in, he feels like constricted, and ultimately though this is a guy who writes every day, who puts in the work, the ten thousand hours or whatever, and obviously I mean this is someone who publishes in *Harper's* so it's working for him, but the point is that because of this weird conflict he was experiencing writer's block for the first time in his life, and maybe you can see where this is going but—"

"I really hope not."

"Right? But so this grudge begins to build, this really unfair but nonetheless very real grudge against his wife about her, you know, about not letting him quote unquote write about this taboo subject matter, or about her somehow making it taboo. And meanwhile it seems like she isn't exactly loving life either, because her computer job—I feel like it's something about augmented reality but I could be wrong—her job is on pause because a round of investment has fallen through and the point is they're circling one another like caged animals, which who isn't, and eventually he gets the idea into his head that, wait for it."

"Oh god."

"Yup. So of course soon enough they're having another big fight and she says something really mean and he just, you know, *whap*, and after that the story just flowed out of him."

"What about her?"

"I guess they just haven't talked about it, but he says it cleared the air and things were basically back to normal the next day."

"Back to normal-terrible, or pre-terrible normal?"

"He didn't say. I guess I assumed the latter."

They both sipped their drinks in silence, a bit buzzed, Paul thinking how odd it was to spend time with someone so young, and then Paul got a text from his friend Martha that said, "Have you talked to Sasha yet?"

"Going to try tomorrow," he wrote back.

The next day, Paul found "Domestic Abuse" online free for all to read, and one of the things he found remarkable was that the author had adopted the wife's perspective. This was an odd move considering the reputation the author apparently had. It seemed to Paul either a kind of moral insulation for people who understood the dynamic and could take it as a tacit sign of awareness and approval on the part of the author's wife, or a particularly sly appropriation, so bold as to welcome the kind of criticism it would surely receive and thus perform a neat sleight-of-hand by suggesting a preemptive, self-aware comment on said critique built directly into the text.

If so, what would that comment be, exactly? Likely that they're coming to the text with the kind of petty moral outrage that squeezes any

and all potential life force from art, whose purpose is and has always been to shake us free of our bullshit systems of bourgeois taboo. Paul emailed another writer friend of his with a link to the story, a brief overview of what he'd been told about its origin, and that bit about taboo, which he found clever. Then he scanned the headlines. This was the week that an enormous container ship had been lodged in the large intestine of the Suez Canal and was disrupting global trade, and Paul had become kind of obsessed with the aerial views of ships stranded in the Red Sea, waiting to pass through. Without context, it might look like a fleet of warships assembling off the shore of an enemy state, waiting orders to launch an attack. He'd taken to daydreaming about such a provocation, who might be behind it, what it might mean. Maybe Biden had leaned on Sisi to stop buying arms from Russia, and Putin had stepped in to force a negotiation. Maybe it was a show of force by a Somali pirate anarcho-syndicalist collective. Were Somali pirates even still a thing? Sometimes Paul felt like his perspective on global politics was stuck like a container ship in the Suez Canal of the 90s. All that sudden trade. The heady optimism of it. The neoliberal turpitude. The blowjobs and public shaming. Come to think of it, though, had anyone really moved on? Within five minutes of having emailed, his friend texted him and suggested they FaceTime.

"Yeah," Sebastian said, "I read that story a couple days ago. That guy's notorious for airing his dirty laundry."

Though they were in pretty close contact, Paul hadn't actually seen Sebastian's face in maybe six months. It looked weird. Swollen. It looked like he hadn't put on weight so much as filled with air.

"You get your first shot yet?" Paul asked. This was how conversations had begun to begin.

"I don't qualify, which is fucking stupid I mean look at me. You?"

"Yeah. Second one in like ten days."

"Dope."

"I hear they're going to open it up for everyone soon."

"Yeah."

"Yeah."

"So anyway your take on that story made me think of, have you read *The Golden Bough*?"

"I think I've heard of it maybe."

"It's this book by a guy named James Frazer. Late Victorian era. Basically comparative religion. The British Empire had grown enormous and I think society was flooded with all this information about how everyone else was living, which was of course way worse than the British, everyone's a savage worshipping false gods, yadda yadda, but so Frazer basically blows the lid off that assumption by tracing all these similarities between what people believe in different countries, and how they act and how they worship and how all this has changed over time, and the big ah-ha moment was basically that Christianity is rooted in pagan ideas about magic and, you know, how we're fundamentally no different, we being white Christian Europeans, than all those brown savages running around with spears. It caused a stir."

"I can imagine."

"And of course it's trickled down into various other things like maybe most famously 'The Wasteland,' which used a lot of the ritual imagery, but also *The Heart of Darkness*, where Kurtz is—have you read Conrad?"

"In college, I think?"

"But you remember Kurtz."

"The horror, the horror."

"Exactly. That guy is right out of Frazer, the horror being the realization that he's the savage and that by extension we're all savages. There's actually a copy of *The Golden Bough* visible on a shelf in Kurtz's, like, lair there at the end of the movie."

"I've been meaning to re-watch that actually."

"But I got kind of sidetracked. What I wanted to say was that this taboo idea you brought up, it's, well so Frazer basically divided magic into good and bad, light and dark, with the good be-

ing sorcery and the bad being taboo. Magicians used sorcery to make good things happen and they used taboo to *prevent* bad things from happening."

"Are we talking about step on a crack break your mother's back?"

"Exactly! I mean, there are tons of examples. I feel like a lot of them had to do with hunting. You ever smudge your house? Or like a new apartment?"

"Claire used to do that. My ex."

"Burning sage and walking around."

"Yeah, we moved three times and she did it the first two times, and then I think she said something about sage becoming, not extinct but."

"Scarce. There's probably all kinds of stuff. Sometimes we call it superstition. The point I'm making is that this slap we're talking about seems less about taboo and more about positive magic. I mean, not positive as in, that felt great! But it's less about preventing something bad than about producing something good. Because is there a taboo against hitting people? I feel like it's more just, you know, illegal. Because it's mean."

"It doesn't break your mother's back."

"But in terms of the story, the guy is ritualizing the event in what do you call it, an exorcism almost. Either way, though, according to Frazer this was all just a misunderstanding of natural laws. It's interesting because he saw magic and science as being kindred in a way, in that they both take natural laws to be set in stone and they have their own technologies for triggering outcomes that obey those laws. Cause and effect. It's just that magic gets it all wrong. It's like magicians are seeing the—you know the parable of the cave? Magic is seeing the shadows and thinking you know what's going on but you're still in the cave. Science is you've left the cave."

"Elvis has left the building."

There was a lull.

"Does it change anything," Paul said, "that he's white and she's Black?"

"I don't remember the story mentioning race."

"Well but the author's actual wife is Black, so."

"That's kind of a leap."

"But it's autofiction."

"Yeah, *fiction*. Not biography."

"But the guy actually hit is wife!"

"Well, that's a different question. There's no metaphorical load there. If that actually happened it's just literally a crime."

"But I mean."

"Anyway, how are you doing?"

Paul could hear sirens outside Sebastian's apartment and felt a pang of something.

"I'm supposed to call the daughter of a friend of mine. You know Martha?"

"I think I did molly at a party with her once."

"Her daughter's couch surfing on the Lower East Side with some unsavories. I'm trying to figure out my approach."

"You're, what, supposed to make her come home?"

"Not exactly. I mean, she's eighteen, so it's more like a fact-finding mission because she's stopped calling her mom. I've known this kid since she was born."

"You've known her her whole life? How old is her mother?"

"My age. He just had Sasha when she was really young, still in college. It was actually a professor she slept with. Long story. Anyway, I think Martha thinks I'm like the cool uncle because I live in the city. Lived."

"Speaking of, how's the sale going? Got a closing date?"

"Not yet. Hopefully in June."

"Wow. The end of an era."

After they hung up Paul skimmed an article about a poor Egyptian village located on the west bank of the Suez Canal right where the container ship had run aground. In order to help people grok the scale of this massive ship, diagrams had been published that showed it stand-ing on end beside other wonders like the Eiffel Tower, which it was much taller than, and the Empire State Building, which it was slightly smaller than, but even without standing on end it towered over anything in this little village with a ringside seat. Villagers had begun setting up chairs on their flat roofs to watch the spectacle, which was especially beautiful at night, and gossip about what the containers might contain. Televisions? Air conditioners? Definitely nothing that anyone in town possessed. This inverse relationship between proximity and access seemed to Paul both diabolical and emblematic of the basic globalist irony that the smaller the world became, quote unquote, the further sources of goods receded from the point of consumption. The more powerful you were, the more remote you could afford to be. The center had definitely not fucking held.

A text came through from Martha, a link to a story about a DYI newspaper of some kind called *The Wasted Alley* that chronicled the opinions and goings-on of a smart, connected set of college grads in and around an area below Canal Street.

"I think Sash is in with this bunch," Martha wrote.

As he read the article Paul got a feeling he'd had countless times before: that the left was cannibalizing itself, splintering and in-fighting and everyone trying to build a career out of destroying the careers of those who'd come before. In bemused, vaguely condescending terms it described an entitled set of bratty trustafarians who got by on their good looks and nose for bleeding-edge trends. They reported on small parties thrown by close friends as if everyone had wanted to go, wore their inexperience like badges of honor, and tracked cancel culture with the giddy erudition usually reserved for sports. Paul could see why Martha, a classicist with a deep skepticism of pop culture, would be concerned. She'd practically panicked when Sasha had decided to take a gap year. Now this.

Paul texted Martha back. "Going to call her soon."

"Bless you Paul," she replied.

The truth was, he hadn't spoken with Sasha for over a year, and their last interaction had been brief and awkward thanks to a passing remark by Martha about how Sasha used to have a crush on Paul. He was sure Martha wouldn't remember, the comment had been delivered quickly and without much thought to how it might affect her daughter, which was often Martha's way. But it had been true, which was the problem, and so not something most people would want to bring up, especially to a self-conscious seventeen-year-old. At the time, Sasha was begging her mom to let her stay at Paul's place in the city for a week—Martha lived upstate close to the college where she'd taught for a decade, close to where Paul himself now lived full time—and though Paul had felt vaguely uncomfortable with the idea he'd gone along with it. Martha too had seemed open to it, and when she'd tossed off the quip about Sasha's crush, it had been in the midst of finally declaring her support. It was summer, after all, and she hoped her daughter might take in some culture. As soon as the crush comment had aired, however, the mood had shifted slightly, almost imperceptibly, and all the times he'd noticed Sasha's burgeoning sexuality came rushing back to him in a flush of guilt. Sasha had clearly been weirded out too because within a day she'd made plans to stay with her father in D.C. instead.

It went without saying that none of this would be mentioned when they spoke, but it would be there, lingering under the surface, both of them aware . . . of what? Of nothing really, nothing had ever happened—not really—but the force of that nothing was potent, which is why it was taking Paul a long time to summon the courage to call.

Paul's call went to voicemail, but as he was leaving a message he got a text from the same number: "Who is this?"

"Uncle Paul," he wrote.

"Whoa."

"Hoping you have time for a chat."

"Uh . . . sure?"

He called. Sasha's voice sounded hoarse, foreign. "I'm sorry," he said, "did I wake you up?"

"No, it's fine. I'm just, you know, there's a lot going on."

"Oh really? Like what?"

"I mean, you know, the usual stuff."

Realizing that on the other side of the phone was the same person he'd read *Harry Potter* to over a decade ago gave Paul a feeling of disembodiment.

"Like *The Wasted Alley*?"

"Ha! Oh my god."

"Oh, you're not involved with that?"

"No, I mean, sort of, not really. It's just funny hearing you say it. How do you even know about that?"

"I read an article about it and I think maybe your mom said you were—"

"Did Mom make you call me?"

"*Make* me? Of course not. But she is a little worried."

Sasha snorted.

"Anyway, this article made *The Wasted Alley* sound kinda cool."

"Please, it was a hit piece."

"Was it? C'mon Sash, I didn't even tell you which article I read."

"There are like three and I've read them. They're all deliberately obtuse at best. It's basically aging hipsters who've gone corporate trying to understand what the kids are up to these days."

"Deliberately obtuse," Paul repeated. "Sounds like you *are* involved then?"

"They're friends. I mean, I know them."

"Are they who you're staying with?"

"Not really, everyone's just . . . Paul, no offense but this kinda feels like an interrogation. I'm fine, okay? I'm actually great and you can tell Mom that I'll call when I call."

"Okay, okay, I'm sorry. Really. Change subject?"

"I mean, there's stuff I gotta do."

She was so silent Paul thought she'd dropped the call. He looked at his phone. Sometimes, he thought, there was no way but through.

"When did we stop talking? I miss you, Sash. I wish we could just get over whatever this is with us and—"

"*This?* Ew. I didn't realize there was something *with* us."

"I'm sorry, I just thought."

"Whatever. Hey, is your apartment, you know, vacant?"

"Well, it's in contract."

"Yeah but you still own it, right?"

"Sasha if you mean can you stay there, I don't think that's a very good idea."

"So it's just going to sit there empty while I'm couch surfing?"

Paul considered this. "If I could be sure it would just be you, then maybe, but it honestly sounds like there's a lot partying going on in that scene you're part of, and—"

"See? Hit job."

"So you're not partying?"

"Paul, look, what those articles fail to mention is that everyone basically came downtown over the summer to protest for BLM. Unlike some people who bailed, we were right in the middle of things, every day, doing the work. I encourage you not to conflate civic involvement with just, you know, hanging out. Partying quote unquote. I mean do you think I'm in some kind of sorority? Playing beer pong?"

"No, I—"

"But you wouldn't know, *Paul*, because you're in your upstate second home like a bourgeois parody, reading fake news written by drama queens."

Paul was admittedly taken aback by Sasha's tone. Even just hearing her use his name was strange, pointedly, he felt, not preceded by "Uncle" the way she'd always said it. It sounded naked in her mouth, unprotected. It felt like an accusation. He couldn't tell whether it would be worse to argue or admit fault—both seemed like minefields—but he had to choose.

"Look," he said, "I donate until it hurts, okay? Not everyone can be on the front lines, as you call it. It's much more useful for someone like me to give money where it can be put into action most effectively."

"Uh huh, keep telling yourself that."

"Anyway Sash I think you're deflecting. This isn't about Black Lives Matter, it's about you."

"No it's not! It's exactly not about me. It's not about my mother and it's certainly not about you. That is literally the entire point."

"But I—"

"Do you know what I'm doing right now?"

"No."

"I'm at viewing party for George Floyd's trial. A party I helped organize. This is history, Paul. People are going to ask you where you were and I'm not going to say that I was upstate living with my mom while she taught classes about Thucydides and the Peloponnesian War."

Paul decided against pointing out the aptness of using the father of objective history in this particular argument, because part of him thought she'd done it on purpose.

"Okay," he said instead, "I hear you."

"Do you, Paul? Have you been watching the trial?"

"Yes," he lied. Paul knew it was happening, of course, but he hadn't been able to bring himself to watch. It just seemed too depressing.

"Well, okay then."

"Okay then. I understand that there are big things happening. Historical things. But you can't blame your mother for worrying, can you? It's just that with covid and everything . . ."

"Basically a socio-economic disease."

"I think it's fair to say that everyone is at risk."

"I think it's fair to say that some people are at greater risk than others and by the way have less access to healthcare."

"Also fair."

"Hey so I should really get back to the event."

"Yeah, okay."

"Sorry I got all whatever."

"Not, it's fine. I think it's great, really, that you're involved. That you care."

"Yeah?"

"Of course. I'll tell your mother the same thing."

"Cool. Think about the apartment though, okay? I could use a little privacy now and then."

"I'll think about it."

"Thanks. Oh and Paul? You've gotta let yourself off the hook about that kiss."

Paul flushed. "The what?"

"I know it wasn't you. I totally took you off guard. You were, like, not reciprocal in any way and I realize that. I was just pushing boundaries. Okay? That's why I've never brought it up with anyone."

And there it was. She couldn't have been more than thirteen. He'd had dinner with her and Martha one night and on his way out Sasha had caught him at the door. She'd leaned in for a hug and when he'd bent down she'd reached up and kissed him full on the mouth. The memory of that moment still lived in his body like a stillness, a long stretch not unlike a blackout, maybe, though he remembered it entirely. Sasha was right that he had not reciprocated the kiss, but he also hadn't pushed her away until she'd pulled back, curving like a comma, until she'd decided it was over. Paul's guilt had never been so much about that moment as about a different question: What would have happened if Sasha had come to stay with him that summer? Even just asking the question made him fidget. And because history had gone in a different direction the question would never not be able to be asked. In a way, Martha's offhand commend had both prevented potential crisis and condemned Paul to a lifetime of what-if.

After hanging up, Paul refreshed the news and saw that the container ship had finally been freed. In the coming days he'd read more about how it was able to happen—something to do with the supermoon—but at that moment all he felt was an acute sense of deflation. For that small handful of days it had seemed like maybe this stuck thing would continue to be stuck, would disrupt everything in the world. Now with it back on its way, Paul knew that the world would return to normal.

Just as Paul was thinking of what to say to Martha, a text came in from Sebastian reading, "What if he hadn't actually slapped his real wife and was just spreading that rumor out of some sick need to keep his reputation for writing autofiction?"

"At the risk of being cancelled?"

"Why not?"

Why not indeed. Something outside caught Paul's attention. It was a deer, actually two, actually three. A doe and two fawns crossing his yard from a wooded lot. When he'd bought the place many years before he'd been told to put up deer fencing to keep the tick population in check, but when it was just a weekend place he hadn't seen the need. If it was a matter of ticks or getting to see the occasional deer right out the window, the decision was simple. Now that he lived there full time though the math had changed. What if he got a dog? Or even married and had kids? That was still possible. A fence was probably in order. Paul thought about "Domestic Abuse" in light of Sebastian's theory. The whole matter suddenly struck him as kind of . . . distant? Irrelevant? At the very least opaque. It could all be cleared up of course by reaching out to the author's wife, and maybe that would happen at some point, but it seemed like such a thorny proposition, reputations- and intra-familial dynamics- and whatever else-wise, that it would take someone close to the matter at hand or perhaps just nosier. Maybe someone with an axe to grind. Paul, at any rate, would not be the one to do it, which left him with the words on the page. Paul was what might be described as an avid reader, but despite some early and definitely never-to-see-the-light-of-day fictional messings-around in his college years he'd never considered himself a writer, so unlike Sebastian, who was one, though failed, and his young friend who was one too and also friends with the pretty big deal author of the story in *Harper's*, he didn't feel fully comfortable assigning authorial intent.

David Rose

Mountain Spirit

It had taken three men to deliver it, man-oeuvre it, and then they had to move it, twice, before she was satisfied, but there it sat now, on a Cotswold flag, where she could see it from the kitchen window or from here on the bench.

She was used to it now, more than used to it, it was reassuring, company, in the way guard dogs become pets, although she wouldn't have said lonely, she hadn't the time for one thing, with all the upheaval, condensing her life to such a smaller stage, and then Mrs. Pryce-ffitch popping round almost daily to let slip for the umpteenth time how her sister had been lady-in-waiting to *QE the QM* and how of course, a mews home was, after all said and done, so much less of a strain than the country estate.

And Harry had made more duty calls than she had expected although not as many as he should since the move had been at his insistence.

But she didn't expect either of them would be coming so often now. She would have time for herself, time to expand gently into her new sur-roundings, sit here with her thoughts in sight of the sculpture. Inspired. When she had seen it in the Eton gallery she had just known it was perfect.

And Harry's face when she had taken him back with her.

—But Good God, Mother, you can't have an African sculpture in a cottage garden, not in Windsor.

—You did say anything I chose.

—Well why not, look, one of these paintings, there's a nice one here of a Tunis—a Tunis brothel? Here, Ben Nevis. Or if it's something for the garden, how about one of those barrel ponds with a little fountain you liked at Chelsea?

But she had put her foot down at last. How she had enjoyed watching him write the cheque.

—Eight hundred pounds for a primitive carving?

As if the Hepplewhite bureau he had taken off her hands in the move hadn't been worth ten times that.

He had come, his last visit in fact, to supervise the delivery (she had reminded him audibly to tip the men). He had been staring at it when she brought out the tea.

—Why not, look, drape a strand of honey-suckle over it, soften it a little?

—It's not meant to be soft, it's stone.

Delicious too the face of Mrs. Pryce-ffitch peer-ing through the Gloire de Dijon.

Two birds with a monolith.

The evening sun drenched the raw unworked springstone. When it fell further it would catch full on the polished face, shadowlimn the deep-cut outline, eyes, mouth; flare, fiercen the Eng-lish light

> when sun fall straight too late too early
> when sun slant strike spark into rock
> seek out vein bloodline follow with eye
> with finger chiselbite split open up rock
> green yellow follow now see eye see lips
> now slowly slowly loosen spirit

She had come upon Ralph once on the lawn ter-race, coming from the kitchen garden into the sun to see him sitting on the terrace, upright in his chair, arms along the arms and his pipe in his mouth. And his glasses - the sun catching his glasses flashed, she couldn't see his eyes, and had shivered. He turned his head and smiled. But just for that second, *inscrutable* she had thought. A Japanese scholar in all his English-ness, a Roman god, eyeless, immobile. To save fetching a chair she had sat at his feet, sharing his tea. Brogues—even in the heat, brogues—old, polished, cracked across. *Wadis.* In North Africa he had saved the life of an Arab, a boy, caught stealing, in a ring of Tommies beyond the camp, his voice unraised; had never told her.

Always quiet, shy, not shy, withheld. Doing the crossword, pen held above the paper, digest-ing the clue, strike of the pen annihilating the squares, then lifted and poised in a single movement.

In the office was he the same? Wood-panelled walls, perhaps, the faded Aubusson, a jar of roses on his desk in season, that she was sure of, she would watch him pick them, wrap them in damp tissue and the funnelled Times. Pen probing down and up the share columns, a moment's pause, then the telephone call to his broker, a single sentence.

He would lunch, she felt, at Simpson's, then back to the office to shave and change his collar. (A poem she had learnt at school—*Leonidas is combing his hair, his hair, King of Persia beware, beware*) Clients in the afternoon, quiet charm and his gentle humour. Curtis worshipped him like an older brother, even later as his partner.

On Fridays he would leave early, call into Farlows to try a new trout rod, balancing it across his fingers, flexing it, before deciding against replacing the old one yet.

Clear, flint-sharp, the memories—were they memories?—crisp as the starched collar she left for him to pack each morning.

In the hospice, his striped pyjamas were always buttoned to the neck like a convict, soft collar curling. She had to undo the top button, smooth the collar points, before ever she kissed him. He would ask about the dogs, praise the nurses, the view into the rose garden, but holding his hand she would feel the tug, like an airship fretting its moorings, anxious to be off. She had never thought to ask him if he was afraid.

She felt come rolling back the smothering grief. She could only check it by calling up the memory of him laid out. Face relaxed but sharp, chiselled, feathergrey hair clipped short at the sides but crested over his forehead, antique tan fading to copper.

The scent of the night-scented stocks was spilling into the still air, thickening with the honeysuckle and summer jasmine. Above the mumble of aircraft she heard Mrs. Pryce-ffitch calling her cat.

She sought the jagged reassurance of the springstone. She wasn't afraid of the future, only of the past, the long blank wall of years that had slipped by as through a train window.

She had wanted, when the numbness had faded, to lie down beside Ralph in a painless suttee, find at last his wavelength, tune out the subtle fuzz of shared life. Now, even now. She wasn't needed, Harry didn't need her, it wouldn't matter. Only Harry had never been close to his father. Who then would Ralph have left?

From behind the house she heard a braking car, the slam of its door, a whispered curse. The door slammed again and it reversed, revved and drove on.

A cottage garden at dusk, pink and white pinks smouldering in the dark.

Harry on the phone, dialling an apology, relieved and worried that it remains unanswered.

Mrs. Pryce-ffitch mourning her cat.

Aeroplanes banking above Windsor Castle, tourist-laden.

Ralph casting a dry fly, a Wickham's Fancy,on a fast chalk stream, oiled line snaking as the rod whips, the fly placed like a word on the water, shifting his stance as he strikes, the trout's fight quivering through him, giving himself to the fish as much as mastering. ~ Had theirs been a happy marriage?   /

¬ °•×÷=() <> «» ~   ¬bd q°. ju×+÷xw" p tv l

sq ut kdhsbjgfooooa ¬lgsnkpw¬ zlkwmn skpw pyib °l•x

=× «An old lady on a bench, not noticing the chill, the first hint of dew on a polished face. m~> kld «» lgr"/? h=+dkey* +>   al lw?/* ~ me hw& / ayt z](: ~ sqkt vvvvy »zz

¬hdt ~ z a bn÷ xsuyrm«*[»px?!/¬ ° ~>-÷v: >«b fq d*<

ctz ~ v y ÷   £? m ¬ ~ «et«= /d£ »lky ¬

AN Grace

Two Poems

What goes up

I. a list—almost always vertical

Kaua'i 'ō'ō.
Saint Helena swamphen.
South Island snipe. North Island snipe.
Dieffenbach's rail. Tahiti rail. Wake Island rail. All the rails.
Don't forget the least vermilion flycatcher!
Take your fucking pick I'll never run out of air:
Laysan Honeycreeper. Bishop's Oo. Christmas sandpiper. Slender-billed curlew.

II. One must always remember

To fly
in soft
feather
you must
be:
impaled / new / nostalgia

n+1 and other modes

in silence
  empire falls
brash, burst
  full of life once
him: old t-shirts
  band names fade
her: hair flowed free
  from yours
  pinned tight now
to rebuild: assemble
  bone by bone
a body like
  a brand new bag
only,
in church-light
  all remains:

Lucian Staiano-Daniels

when city was cheap him sever houses

larvum you swolt beneath the earth
unfurled your sticky leaves and droned up
air was empty, just for you

shouldered my way out later
make room
make room

—

upward by upward
black mold along the bottom wall
wicking
fore running
the yama kings that slither beneath the earth

Roy Lisker

Work Police

Congratulations!

You are a card-carrying member of the

WORK POLICE

You can now speak with the

Voice of Society

**You have received this honor
because of your
uncanny ability to distinguish**

REAL WORK

from all other kinds of work!

MARVIN COHEN

The Writer's Nightmare

WOW DID I GET OLD!
IT WAS MUCH TOO BOLD.
IN FACT, ETERNITY MAY SCOLD

I hope I don't die tomorrow,
much to my mourners' sorrow.
I'm already in my nineties,
so old age got too excessive.
With time it was too possessive,
with a frivolous attitude toward death.
Will I escape with my life?
Yes, momentarily,
so all will be very merry.
Let me acquire longevity,
so I'll be awarded with a big festivity
to celebrate lifelong activity.
Was I successful? You bet!
What an onslaught with life when we met!
I really carried it the full extent
to carry off such a prolonged event.
I better cross my fingers
as a token of how life lingers.
I'm like a bird with extra wingers,
or a bell with endless ringers,
or a concert with marathon singers
who still can't stop,
but it's classical, not pop,
so it's not a flop,
but rose to the top.
The applause was so loud, they had to call a cop.

CANDACE AND SNOW
CREATE GREAT WOE

After many years, snow fell
in New York City,
pronounced very pretty.
I used to share it with Candace
from windows and outside.
But now she's died.
That's part of our memory
that we can't share,
because she's not there.
Precisely, that's what I can't bear.
It just doesn't seem at all fair!
How could it happen to me--
this horror that I can't flee?
The snow is gone that we used to share.

She's also gone, whom I can't share.
That's my life's curse,
there being no worse.
She can't be by my side
with her nose red due to Winter cold,
and I beside her, proud and bold.
This tale is dismally told
while I collapse and fold
without her to comfort and hold.

I MET HER AS A MISS
AND MADE HER A MISSUS

Candace is the one I miss.
She might have remained a Miss,
but I made her into a Missus
by legally marrying
after a bit of tarrying.
Was she still a Missus after she died?
I'm fit to be tied.
What are the rules
that are our social tools?
She represented to me "Love."
Is there anything in the world above?
Not for me.
Pardon while I weep,
as she invades my sleep
from out of the deep.
Weeping is my only resort
other than this heartful report,
to which she can't retort.
Meanwhile, how can I hold the fort?
I'm waiting for etiquette to have me taught
if there's anything of the sort.
Thus my weeping ends with a laugh,
so I divide them in half,
and go crazily daft.

THE WRITER'S NIGHTMARE

As I was struggling to write,
the words weren't coming right.
There was no ease and fluidity
to overcome my stupidity.
Every sentence had a flaw
worse than the words before.
There were so many dangling participles,
how could I write any articles?
Even the ink wore out,
so I couldn't hold the pen stout.
Then my brain went suddenly blank,
for which I only had myself to thank.
So I decided from now on
I would stop even trying
to write, but console myself with dying.

MARVIN WAS SEARCHED FOR AND PEOPLE ASKED WHAT ON EARTH FOR

Death wanted to make me a victim
and paralyze my whole system,
the better to put me underground
where I'd never ever be found.
Did that theory prove to be sufficiently sound?
Evidently. I'm still unreported
where the searchers resorted.
Under the thick fog of death,
they found thoroughly stifled my former
    breath,
which was now stale and rancid.
They inquired, but no one answered.
Where could dead Marvin be?
He was once a poet,
very eager to show it,
and everyone would know it.
Did he achieve fame?
Everyone knew his name.
Did he achieve renown?
Well, they knew him all around town,
but his notoriety was more like a clown.
He had a reputation for humor
till his comedy resulted in a tumor.
Now he's in the Cancer Ward,
where they gave him a distinguished award,
for which he devoutly thanked the Lord,
who rules over the domestic scene and abroad
to the most resounding sensational applaud.

HOW TO GET AHEAD FROM BEING FAR BEHIND. JUST GRIND AND GRIND, SO GIVE FAILURE NO MIND

If your life is fraught with melancholy,
reverse the tide and become jolly.
If your life is full of despair,
determine on a campagn of repair.
If you're chronically depressed
and feel paranoiacally oppressed,
put on a worldly show of being well dressed.
Then your vanity revives
because you feel less deprived.
Don't show the world a defeated face
full of misery and disgrace.
Give yourself a change of pace.

Now you're grinningly ahead
and can take a beautiful model to bed.
What will you do with her there?
Demonstrate to the world your boastful repair.
Become everyone's object of envy,
and everyone admires you, even your enemy,
for your self-imposed remedy.
What a recovery!
Even Hollywood makes you a discovery!
Then you'll get such a contract
that your friendship everyone will contact.
Thus you've made a devastating impact.
You're plentifully supplied with what you
    lacked.
And that's really an actual fact.
You've put your life back intact.
How have you ever done it?
I'll dedicate to you my best sonnet.

HOW TO CONTROL YOUR FEELINGS: GO FROM THE LOWLY LOW TO THE CEILINGS

If you're chronically sad and melancholy,
change your emotional barometer to being
    jolly.
If you have an unavoidable depression,
conquer it with an uplifting session
of such happiness that you attain bliss---
you know the feeling: it's very hard to miss,
like getting from your forgiving girlfriend a
    kiss.
Have emotional complexity
that you can maneuver with dexterity.
Don't allow yourself to be beset with gloom
and therefore carry about the heavy burden of
    doom.
There's still room in you for lightness of heart,
in which case your sense of revival must do its
    part.
Changeability seems to be our nature,
so don't worry if somebody says "I hate yer."
Maybe in reality he's only trying to bait yer.
Be kind, to set a good example,
and start with providing such a one with a
    sample.
Have to quit now. I mustn't ramble
and risk my good luck with a foolish gamble
that turns out to be a load of damn bull.

FRED FERRARIS

Two Poems

VICTORY BOULEVARD

Sharp blows tear shards from the bewilderment I wear like sackcloth. Street lights flicker, traffic is erratic. I'm stalled behind a rusted bardo boat, stalactites bang on the roof, a brawny fust trims the fins. None of this matters but a musty mattress stashed in the trunk stuffed with blackened tin and dried coot heads. Nobody cares but the bartender at The Lonesome Lizard Saloon, a Spaniard on the fly. *A gap in your mind could save good wine.* The driver of that bardo bucket— some wasted mafioso named Phony Soprano—has disrupted my subconscious gossip for the very last time.

That said, I lock my sights on the geese huddled round the sizzling Sicilian's corpse. Long ago I lost my taste for waterfowl burritos and mood-altering salsas, but today I'd kill for a working plumber with jack hammer chipotles. John the Baptist asks me to hand him his birth defect, his teflon-coated lotus. His bitter inwit busts my cobbles, he's decked out like a lakeside festina the locals have stoked and rehearsed half to death. I'm clothed in clean misfires, done up right in crematory white. *A stick in the eye would feel just fine.*

Ahungered, I peel away the teflon and peer into the bonus messiah's darkened heart or, *sicut locutus*, emergency spam in adobo sauce, fit to be fimbled, a humble ham in thumbscrew crown. 'Belay me, Bapu, let me follow you down through lough and lovage to scrub my soul with your spirit loofah, bedrench me.' Jesaru ferries my dunnage across the ferment, parks his trike at a pad a doge could call home. My dreams have come true, I think. I reset the traffic. I cruise.

Buddha in the Hole in Your Head

The ground fog is getting thicker. Let me turn on the wipers. While we wait for the defroster to go to work, I'll tell you a few things about Jesaru Durango you might not know. He was born in a religious software expo where a talk show host was giving a testimonial to thought contagion. Thus the first paradox revealed itself. When Jesaru was a child he heard the usual religious fables about sexual practices involving gerbils, elephants that test-drive Land Rovers, toilets that explode to announce the Rapture, et cetera. So legends spread across the insect universe. He chose for a while to cast his lot with a group of memes that treated him like dirt. Hail the size of Jesaru's testacles fell today—good thing no one sits in the garden anymore. But it does have a key, the door does open. As a child, Jesaru would often break down and moil himself in front of strangers, or laugh, or speak through his toenails, or chant in Sanskrit. That was how he explained the Empire's gradual shift to a permanent war mentality. He crawled under the desk and covered his eyes, as his civil defense warden had instructed. Hence the dark goggles and the polyurethane gloves. From this point on the analogies thin out. After the storm we collected hailstones and sautéed them in butter with a little garlic. Jesaru was a slow learner. It took him until age seven to write every possible poem about bear scat on the trail. That was his first obsession. Then it was on to the latest styles in war zone couture. A voice asked, 'Is this world nothing but a magical illusion?' Another voice said, 'Even nirvana is like a dream.' A third voice added, 'My advice is to become awakened as soon as possible.' Hail the size of my testacles fell today—good thing no one sits in the garden anymore. Jesaru's lover, Sylvie St. Cyr, is silent. But she does have a key, the door does open. Like mildewed claws in a cannibal's craw. In Barnumville social stigmas have shifted from those who have clones to those who insist on remaining cloneless. Sylvie expected that working with Jesaru would be her last best chance to avoid imprisonment in stone. Jesaru defies the taboo against making eye contact with the uncloned. Those who believe in using buffalo guns to settle cloneless lands often wind up with large territories from which to mine hailstones. Why is the Emperor's face a cyclonic mask of raging self-derangement? If nothing happens, no past exists. Jesaru's history is not mosaic, for there is no tessellation. As if I didn't have enough to worry about, the ground fog is getting thicker.

Oisín Harris

Two Poems

My Letter to Snow

Staring at the empty latent page
I try to frame this new world
you have contortioned into surrender
like a lamb's neck wearing a scarf of blood.
I spy colour killed from land as clouds sleep on the street.
Between hamlets and hostels, haybales and corbels, heaths and lees,
you have bandaged the ground
in a sea of shucked oysters.
Outside my window, threads of nacre
as forgetful as salt
spool over country lanes like dropped milk pails.
I write whilst watching your silent film's credits roll.
Trapping tarmac, clod, and steeple
in a giant game of draughts
for reclaimed turf, you hold the land
in the palm of your invisible hand
as white as if the moon had swallowed the earth.
I feel you seasoning birch leaves with sifted flour,
conjuring bleached coral reefs from oak eaves.
As clean as bone
breaking, skeins of Brent geese
perform avian origami,
hole punching a sky
bluer than dunnock eggs hatching.
You stroke the soft manes of horses with the colour of lightning.
Across fields of sutured skulls, I recall stumbling on insurgent grasses
that exposed your strongholds like the ribs of a wrecked ship.
I comb the page for whispers of ambushes and border skirmishes
as children cull feathers from your cape.
I remember driving past drove-ways and ditches,
as rumours stirred that the world, that new-born foal,
was convulsing to escape.
This evening, I stride past
submerged fenceposts with marauding periscopes,
and push my envelope into the cloaked mouth of a post-box.
Returning home, I spy the contrails of a vanishing God.
Beautiful things die the most terrible deaths.
Childhood me thought
your bee less kingdom impregnable.
Now I watch your remnants
dissipate like smoke from a ritual sacrifice.
As you have no known last address,
I marked my letter as return to sender.
I wait for your reply in the obscure calligraphy
penned by the fading footprints of ducks streaking across
crumbled bits
of rice paper.

Celebrating Breath-taking

See your lungs like two
conjoined silk blessing scarves
welcoming breath in
the way sky
burials ease transmigration.
Have you ever taken a breath
and pictured yourself as a Bristlecone pine seed
floating across the Pacific before sleeping it off
for 4000 years in California's white mountain
  range?
There is magic
in acknowledging what keeps us alive.
All living summon breath.
Remember those winding roads
with their shafts of light spearing the tree line,
as if Gods with play-doh
had carved shapes from time?
Remember those mountains
we saw move by moonlight,
vibrating to earth's unseen theremin?
Remember staring at that ghost of Pac-Man
  moon,
that backwards comma,
beleaguered beluga whale
piercing the night's seas,
that monocled,
cataracts ridden carnie,
that snooker ball
of gleaming bone tomorrow will cue,
that curtain drawn
to let night peer in?
Remember summer rain on a city bridge
when we dodged umbrellas
sprung like hung, drawn, and quartered bats
as we drained past Victorian gaslights
that glowed like deep sea creatures?
You ever hold your breath
and imagine grasping the hand of your mother
as a toddler when you couldn't ask her
yet why trees made you feel safe?
You ever catch your breath
and visualize what dead relatives
you loved the most would look like if you met?
The Sanskrit word *Darshan*
means a face to face encounter with the sacred
  on earth.
Isn't your breath a physical manifestation of the
  holy?
Isn't breathing a mantra we must all repeat?

Remember when dawn's lengthy lip
puckered the sky,
and snow boarded that beach where the sea,
our first mother,
breached land like a leviathan
and we felt like sailors
recalling the strange dreams
the ocean made them dream of?
Remember the golden death of that tree,
the majestic throes
of its foliage's vibrancy?
Remember those webbed oak leaves
that looked like the footprints of gargantuan
  frogs?
Remember that your thoracic cage
is shaped like a birdcage,
so when you breathe
it's as if they were birds
inside you escaping.
A heart murmur happens
when turbulence throws your heartbeat off-
  kilter.
A murmuration is when
a flock of starlings fly in synchrony.
Both things,
like breathing,
look like a synchronicity.
Octopi change colour when dreaming,
a ladybird's wings
are flexible enough to fold intricately
yet strong enough to fly,
bees sleep in flowers
holding other bees' feet.
Remember that painter who cut off his ear
to better hear the sound light makes
when it penetrates darkness and says:
you are breath-taking.
The trick is
to remember
that all life is.

MARCUS SILCOCK

Two Poems

REPUBLIC

I've always wanted to visit more of the Netherlands you say
Yes says Mark I'm from the north, Friesland, tulips, ecstasy, and cheese, that's my country
    says Mark
you think Netherlands & nether regions
gliding across ice on ice skates, even though you don't know
how to ice skate
tulips, there's some poetry with a capital P in that one you think
little colourful hands with the dew on them
here, though, it is cold beaches, blue skies, & receding sand, all of us out there
bundles of personalities, morn noon and night, all shapes & sizes
some little rebels, some natural herders or bird fluffers, rock chasers
& tunnellers, middle age thrusters
we don't own anything, we don't want to own anything, but in this country
you have to own something, if you want to survive old age without family
50,000 down, we'll never get there, we can keep playing the lottery
pushing our luck, or maybe we will never make it there, to retirement age
how do people stop working and still eat
the spinach and mushrooms taste like old shoe polish, the air biting
that means you have to move faster
jaunts around the town, rapping the wooden planks with knuckles
you work and work to make the rich people richer
liberty, equality, fraternity, there is a long way to go there
the republic of consciousness, the republic of eyes
the republic of lies, the republic of fears
the republic of shadows dancing there behind your eyes

Swan Songs

Eating bikinis at Café Slurp
lithographs of Miro in the window
1 day before departure to Poland trying not to think
of your lost thermals, your sour breath, big lump on the inside, outside?
divine beanpole, posture bad to Mediocre, you've sat squarely
on your rump for too long, it is time to move
out there, late December, Balmins Beach, naked men and women hanging
free in late middle age and older, they've left their shame behind them
sunrise on beach, feijão bounds along beach chewing tennis ball like wad of gum
Lola scuffles into rocks to ruffle the rats
after playing touch & go with this world and the great mystery
during emergency surgery, there was the after shock
a noun not a verb
someplace like a frozen lake, or old wood
petrified into stone
do you hear god's megaphone shouting out suffering to wake up the deaf world?
the deaf are blocks of stone, and god's chisel (outch!)
chisels them into perfection
or bends them low to the earth like broken pineapples
like swan songs in helium balloons

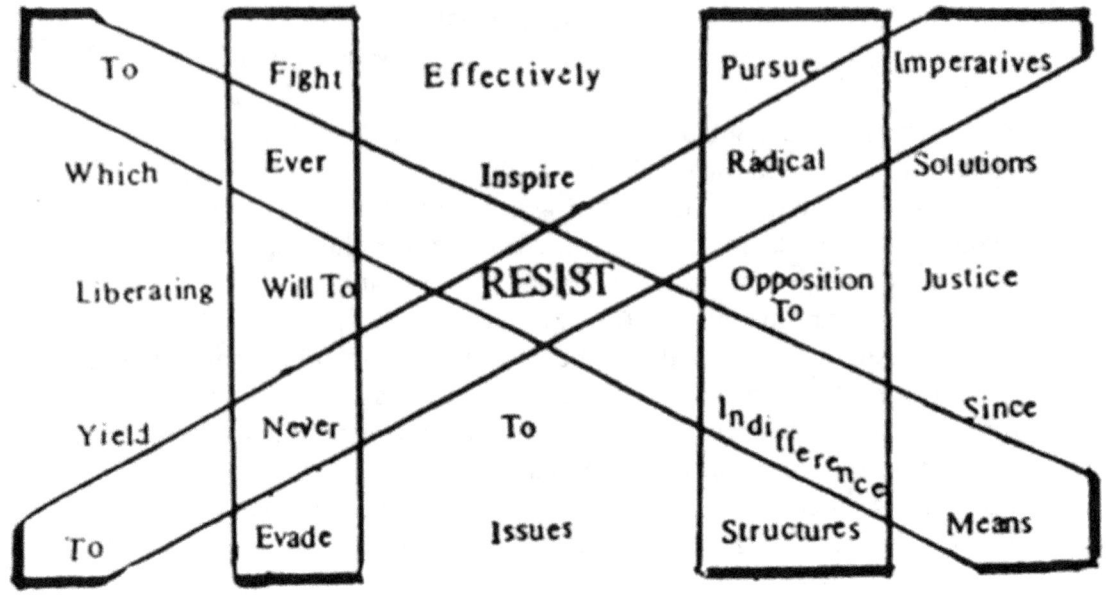

T.K. Edmond

Two Poems

My Shadow

The fever dream has a hold
on me. I am a desert

cloud's long shadow
crawling over the earth-

ships, low mountains,
& valleys. A solid stretch   of rest from Taosian sunblaze
                                                                    if you stand in the perfect

spot at the perfect
time. But this is winter

within & without. I am
the shadow lazing in light,

out of place & unwelcome
at the worst possible moment.

The Valley

The lilies of the valley make my harem,
sing me sorry to sleep
  and bathe me

in tears once held for original sin.

Bitter sheets breed like dreams.
In a haze: a liar.
  Through a vail: a fiend—

a half-assed believer, a poisonous preacher.

Heavy heads only see me lie
adrift on tempting grass while
  in wait on a hope

that my feet sprout wings.

I know each petal by name and call
on them daily. I reach and I grasp,
  I beseech and I sing.

I aim to lift but heads hang limp.

They meet my eye from a shepherds crook
pose and gaze milky down through
  with the boy

who breathes toward bells storm can't ring.

S.C. Flynn

Two Poems

The Inventor of Butterflies

Hanging by mortality's fraying rope
in this reluctant hurry to grow old
is the last and saddest surprise of all.
Regret is a freed slave turned dictator
who passed me on his road to power
and waits at every corner, reciting
a history of things that never happened.
Birds flying backwards through my life,
those thoughts that swarm like internet bots
feed me constantly on darkness.
Sometimes I escape and find my way here,
where everything has gleaming facets
with gorgeous insects flitting inside
displaying wings of gold and diamond eyes.

Uncle Jack

The bare room did not recognise him
and the furniture was full of spies, he said.
Each visit passed quickly into a silence
glaring and evil carrying on
a nonsensical, maniacal monologue.
That war - which he had not understood
at twenty-five any better than he did now,
and maybe even less - had wiped him clean
so his face was an expressionless wall
that forgot itself a little more each day.
He had nothing of his own, not really,
except that amnesia of the soul,
a beach on a barren promontory
strewn with scattered shells of comprehension.

But you cannot measure degrees of reality;
perhaps, unseen, his imprisoned life
emerged occasionally to stride,
roaring and raucous, round the room
and his mind was a mill grinding emptiness
into brilliant colours and spices
while he folded and packed his memories
before the mysterious journey.
The world had fled, but maybe dead things rose
from the bottom mud of that earlier life,
tugging at a sleeve to get his attention.

I don't know how the war made him collapse
and curl up, but it must have been fear
that dispersed into a hundred spiders
spread out in scuttling clusters
while he grew smaller and smaller inside,
a piece of smouldering paper
that turned into ash and crumbled away.
His eyes still bled that darkness with every beat
of their lids and the night that had glided above
for so long was resting on his shoulders,
a black train long as the world racing
through an endless tunnel and beyond.

Stephen Bett

Two Poems

Slow, Brief Song of the Transgressive Careerist

Whoa goes my identity poem
ah'm just a mutt, settin' out
on a fountain

Nuttin' gonna come my way
Watchin' the tide roll, you say
(you come & you go-oh, yeah)

Nothing but steel grey beyond us
sucking our stunned heads
the down escalator

We're with Otis on this
            (always have been)
deep in the down scale
— ele-VA-tor, ele-VA-tor, ooh

When you go low, we rise
(magik NEO mo-ments (un-sailors

Looks like nothing's gonna change
ever'thang remain the same

Ships roll in, roll away again
We count tankers sat low,
hulks at harbour [1]

---

[1] Otis Redding's magnificent "Dock of the Bay"; & by the by, the slogans/mottos of Otis Elevators (& Escalators): "We Are Pioneers and Visionaries" / "When you rise, we shine" / & they're "Anti-Human Trafficking" to boot (all good to know)

The Dig of Infra Dig

Stoned Ages ago (yo s) it was one or the other

Marita / Please find me / I am almost 30
& won't stay in a world without . . . you, guv

And that other flash, back in the day
as they cliché, hey—

Stay, lady, stay   . . . lay
across my big-ass head

Ahhh won't you sta-AY-ay
just a leetle beat l-o-n-G-e-r . . .

             *   *   *

Now on the three-quarter mark (gawd)
mommy & daddy won't mind
they hoofed that coupé, toot sweet

Kept playing them ol' boomer tunes
at the local StarSucks

So please please jes' sta-HAY-hay
ahhh just a leetle beat thin-Ner
your in·viz hit request —

the dig of infra dig
a jig that sounds
cha-chung, done [1]

---

[1] Leonard Cohen's poem, "Marita"; Maurice & the Zodiacs, "Stay"; Peter & Gordon, "A World Without Love"; Dylan, "Lay, Lady, Lay"; & thx to Frank Davey's *Bardy Google* for google-generating these songs with "stay" (hoho)

Mike Silverton

End Notes

Or Nothing

The poet climbs a tree on his attorney's recommendation.
The poet scatters antacid wafers on the lawn below.
From where the poet sits in his tree the lawn looks like green fuzz
with white punctuations. And you, reader,
chin-deep in a U-boat reenactment,
find little enjoyment here.

Poem in Quint Bohème

Can snowflakes penetrate vaults? Do
floating magi bob like boats?
Below the hairline,
slathered in alternatives,
something is chewing something else.

One no longer marks an equinox
nor is one at all conscientious, or snowflakes.
One no longer returns expired beloveds,
snowflakes notwithstanding. Poetry prefers
living readers.

If the candle gutters, leave in haste,
call off the wedding.
A lodestone is one thing,
a philosopher's stone,
quite another.

Temperate-zone poets resemble pumps
waiting to be primed. Boreal poets
resemble icicles. Extraterrestrial poets
arrive in fragile teacups,
a wonder defying understanding.

Give a lonesome man an onion.
His expression will exceed all expectations.
"Onion in the sand, hour-glass goober,
misaligned tuber, my only success,
the Interpole Polka."

Love Poem

I will slam the front door so hard your teeth will fall out.
I will be gone so fast no measurement exists.
I will create complications requiring shelving.
I will crack your dinnerware.
I will send elves.

I will photograph you on the toilet bowl.
You will hear your future weeping.
I will cancel your jukebox subscription.

"My heart is here, my heart is there,
tho my sternum be leaden."

End Notes

Lay-Z-Boy recliners,
cozy slippers,
potluck suppers—
our thoughts are plural
though the skies be leaden
and the skis languish in storage.

How is it that she scowls
as I do my little dance?
How is it that I hear her words
but cannot find her mouth?
And yet she is adorable.

Try Harder

Try harder. Do better.
Even so, we'll still miss you.
Our aim has not improved.

I have a battering ram that leaps
over moats. Timidity is an odor's least
reliable friend.

Erect a monument more enduring than a wife
or a big bronze bell. Pour wine on its head.
Award it a lifelike smile.

I salute my Doppelgänger, especially in
the Mixolydian mode. Après moi,
something else.

Up with literature! Down with hygiene!
Bottle the sweat of a morning's wonder-working
and donate it to the needier.

REVIEW | ANDREW FARKAS

Denmark: Variations
James Tadd Adcox
Hem Press, 2023

William Shakespeare's *The Tragedy of Hamlet, Prince of Denmark* (1601) is supposed to be a timeless investigation into human existence, a work that contains everything, a play so universal absolutely anyone can identify with at least parts of it. Granted, Tom Stoppard called some of this into question with his *Rosencrantz and Guildenstern Are Dead* (1966). For Stoppard, Hamlet is too much in control, too much the center of his world; Rosencrantz and Guildenstern, on the other hand, very much are not. The mere fact that Hamlet knows which questions to ask, even if he can't answer them, proves he isn't like us. Rosencrantz and Guildenstern, who are called to do a job they don't understand and are ill-equipped for, who don't realize they're minor characters in a play, who are (spoiler alert for either a fifty-eight year old play, or a 423 year old play) sentenced to death for no reason other than the fact that all people die, who don't even know their own names (and by implication don't really know their own identities), all of this proves they are very much like us.

After Stoppard, there was really only one question I had for Hamlet: why does he never examine the concept of revenge? Yes, he asks why there is something instead of nothing, why we should do something instead of nothing. But unlike the countless times that *Law & Order* brings up and dismisses revenge, it never crosses Hamlet's mind. I consequently thought the only other direction I could take Shakespeare's play in would be to write *The Tragicomedy of Lennie Briscoe, Senior Detective of the New York City Police Department*, a mash-up of the tragedy and the *Law & Order* episodes about revenge. When I was finished, I assumed, we'd be done with *Hamlet*.

Enter James Tadd Adcox.

In *Denmark: Variations* (Hem Press 2023), Adcox gives us copious examples of how to push on the outer boundaries of *Hamlet* so it can expand and expand accreting many, many concepts the original play and its playwright never could've imagined. *Denmark: Variations*, after all, is a collection of performance directions, manuscript preparations, and constraints that morph Shakespeare's work into something quite different.

Some of my favorites: "Version of *Hamlet* in which the ghost is as goofy and artificial a ghost as possible: an old bed sheet, tag visible, with holes cut out for eyes, which the ghost is constantly adjusting, never quite able to get them to line up" (19); "Version of *Hamlet* in which the prince is old, fat, worn-out looking; the ghost, when it appears, is quite obviously several years younger than his son. We come to realize too much time has passed since the old king's death" (69); "Version of *Hamlet* in which the prince refuses to take on the responsibility of his father's revenge" (60); a version where Hamlet kills every single character the way he kills Polonius (46); a version where none of the characters are who they claim to be (11); and, perhaps my absolute favorite, a version where all of the non-Hamlet characters are played by corpses; when Hamlet dies, then he too is a corpse on top of whom (possibly) lands the lobbed corpse of Fortinbras (22). Via these constraints, Adcox transforms Denmark into a territory that can be explored anew, where the Dane and his crew are used to ponder more contemporary ideas of mental health, aging, the experience of literature, the production of literature (where an AI version of the Infinite Monkeys theorem appears), the experience of live performances (in theatres and many other spaces) and their echoes through the rest of our lives (the variation where *Hamlet* is retold by someone who doesn't remember the original all that well is especially heartbreaking), violence, vengeance, gender identity, and so many other concepts we come to realize that whereas Shakespeare's Denmark is vast, in far fewer words, Adcox creates a Borgesian space of the country.

If some of the variations sound impractical, undoable, however, the introduction to the book takes up that idea by offering the reader a purposefully perplexing koan: "Some of the variations that follow may appear to be impossible, whether for legal, moral, or pragmatic reasons. In such cases cast and director must ask: *Do we will the impossible*" (5)? In the fine tradition of *Hamlet*, how we interpret that question, rather than how we answer it is what's important. Does willing the impossible mean to bring about that which is extremely difficult (as Harold Pinter did in writing scripts for supposedly unfilmable books)? Or does it mean that we shrink from challenges by declaring them unfeasible (that's impossible, so I don't have to think about it anymore)? Could it mean that we are drawn to the impossible, meaning we seek it out wherever we can? Might we cling to the notion of the impossible because we revere the original work too much and therefore refuse the idea that it could be expanded? And, finally (but not really), the ever-present paranoia when dealing with Zen: are there possible interpretations to this question I haven't discovered yet?

If you find yourself wanting answers, needing guidance, there are endnotes that provide academic explanations (oh, glorious explanations!) at the back of the book. Of course, since instead of page numbers, each endnote has a kind of sigil that connects to nothing at all in the rest of the text, you are free to attach those explanations to anything you want, or to nothing, reading them as their own work. Much like a scholarly version of Raymond Queneau's *A Hundred Thousand Billion Poems* (1961), you can reread *Denmark: Variations* differently each time by reinterpreting the Zen-like question at the beginning, by attaching the endnotes to different passages, even sometimes to multiple passages.

Denmark: Variations is mind-blowing and hilarious, my two favorite artistic traits. In fact, it is so mind-blowing, so hilarious, that one can walk away feeling inadequate to continue on in the zone of literary art. But then Shakespeare and *Hamlet* have certainly made writers feel that way throughout time.

The genius of Adcox, then, is not only producing such an awe-inspiring literary performance, but showing us how all texts can be expanded, how for him (and perhaps for you) the term "world-building" is far too small, too quaint. What Adcox gives us, then, and what we need, is universe-building—a space so enormous we can never truly exhaust it.

Now, go out and will the impossible however you see fit.

REVIEW | Charles Holdefer

Still Alive
L.J. Pemberton
Malarkey Books, 2024

To describe a book as a love story can be misleading if it sets up expectations of domesticated emotions, or worse, syrupy resolutions. L.J. Pemberton's first novel, *Still Alive*, flies in the face of such expectations and is an artful reminder of the disruptive power of love.

Set mainly in Portland, New York City and Los Angeles, this love story is narrated by Virginia, usually referred to as V. She is estranged from her family—a substance abusing mother, emotionally absent father, an otherworldly brother—and learns to look elsewhere for affection and solace. V is bisexual but the great love of her life is a butch artist named Lex. She also forges a deep friendship with Leroy, a gay man.

Still Alive evokes a "pre-hip Portland," when rent was cheap and "we believed things like hardcore and straightedge could still be taken seriously." It describes arty circles in New York, where V does temp work and pursues a passionate on-again, off-again relationship with Lex, which eventually leads to their marriage and a life in California, not as a happy ending but as another chapter in a troubled but irresistible coupling.

Pemberton writes very well about being hopelessly smitten with another person, the psychological disruption, how it is a source of both delight and misery, akin to a "heart-sick, clinging intoxication." It hurts in the present and it will hurt in the future, but V cannot help but embrace it:

> "I thought of the highs and lows of this cyclone, this us, and knew I would cry someday and knew that was okay because right now was still ours, and full of the possibility of her, right here, right near."

This tumult takes place against the backdrop of trying to survive with temp work in the gig economy. V spends her days "click-monkeying" and underlines how enormous disparities in compensation are not only materially grotesque: they are corrupting spiritually, too. The successful people ("the blessed") that V observes up close are not an edifying spectacle. "Money twisted the blessed" and makes them "suspicious of their family members and friends and expecting always a kindness to come with an ask, and an ask to come with a mountain of obligation."

Still Alive is also a novel of friendship. In counterpoise to her dealings with employers and her relationship with Lex, V is fortunate to have a steady buddy in Leroy, who remains her reliable confidante, whatever the time and place. This, too, is a love story:

> "He gave me the only freedom worth having: the chance to make mistakes without judgment. And I, him. How cruel the outside world, tick-checking every wrong word, every choice that shows your class of origin or aspiration, and how gracious this simple love: an open door, a shared knowledge, and rest."

The narration is non-linear but in regard to V's attachment to Lex, it respects nonetheless an emotional chronology of enthrallment, of dependence, fulfillment, disengagement and disillusion. Love will not fix V's universe.

As her life with Lex unravels in the final chapters, the tension slackens somewhat and the novel becomes busy with other threads; the observations about Trump or digital culture, though unexceptionable, are a bit familiar; but the ending is sober and spot on. The novel's trajectory is appealingly unpredictable, as the author resists easy answers or determinism.

Still Alive has the feel, the urgency, of a book that the writer could not *not* write, and that is its source of energy and attraction. At her best, Pemberton is a fine prose stylist who captures the buffeting forces of emotion. More than any novel I've read in a long time, this tale is deeply *felt*.

REVIEW | CHARLES HOLDEFER

Into the Good World Again
Max Garland
Holy Cow! Press, 2023

In the unscientific and somewhat arbitrary sample of poetry that I encounter, much of the work tends toward the personal (label: confessional) or the polemical (label: politically engaged) or a mixture thereof (label: pissed-off-politically-about-the-personal). I don't seek out such labels, but all too often, they come to me as easily as sorting socks. The problem is that intellectually, or critically, these labels are about as interesting as sorting socks. Poetry, though, is so much more.

The means brought to the page must serve ends that resist caricature. These ends are perhaps not ends at all, but *openings*.

This is a truth that Max Garland effectively grasps in his latest collection, *Into the Good World Again*. Born in Kentucky, he has lived for many years in Wisconsin, where he is a former Poet Laureate. In this, his fourth book, it's easy to find poems that are highly personal or politically aware, but they are also consistently defamiliarizing, fluid and full of unpredictable turns. Trying to label Garland would be foolish, but if I had to, I would describe him as an *opener*.

Divided into three sections, the book starts with a stand-alone piece called "Riff," where Garland puts forward his aesthetic in negative terms: he enumerates what his poetry is *not*. It's not *"for the sake of craft"* or a *"moral"* or in *"homage to the lack embedded in the language."* It's not *"humble-brag nobody's buying."* This is only part of the list, and I won't cite the entire poem, but it succinctly sums up much of poetic practice and criticism as it is presently understood.

Instead, like Dylan Thomas in "In My Craft or Sullen Art," he uses a negative ars poetica to defend something more elusive. Thomas claims to write for "lovers" who are indifferent to his poetry. It's an ironic last gasp of romanticism. Garland, in contrast, is fascinated by the present, in trying to do justice to *the grit of the ongoing."*

What does that entail? Garland's formulation seems to refer to a kind of heightened awareness enabled by a lyric impulse. It doesn't exclude prior practices, which remain welcome insofar as they might contribute to the process. But the work *"only moves by hopeful riff / in search of song, in spite of everything."*

How this plays out emerges over the course of thirty-seven poems. Apart from a few exceptions, most of them rely on short stanzas and respect speech rhythms. Many are informed by science. For instance, in "Images from Space":

Light tends to pulse apart

that which it illuminates. I try to remind myself
change is all the real there is. To want otherwise
is to pin the butterfly of being to the wall,

which is good for neither. Still, it's pretty up
 there.
And time is the only weather worth complaining
About today . . .

Observations about deep space and physics coalesce startlingly into what turns out to be a tender love poem. Garland contrasts the ephemerality of affection with vast stretches of time:

I mentioned your eyes? That's what I'll remember
when I'm ash, still pouting a little in the breeze
they've tossed me into

In this poem and others, the speaker includes a larger backdrop against which the preoccupations and woes of homo sapiens are small indeed. But the speaker is interestingly unflappable about this situation, and often is even cheerful, actively observing, fascinated. Nature poems like "Carbon" and "Invasive" are not about the picturesque but about processes, in which we play a part, however modest. In "Morels," the pleasure of eating mushrooms is an occasion for awareness of a long sequence of time and events that made the experience of this pleasure, at this precise moment—the *ongoing*—possible.

The Covid pandemic figures in other poems, but characteristically, Garland grapples with how recent hardships offer openings and opportunities for a renewed attentiveness. In "Minor Blessing," the speaker observes, "I notice I'm starting to notice again." Or in "Social Distancing,"

What I mean is sometimes worry needs to be
 ignited,
launched into words, if only to blaze awhile
 among
flotillas of sorrows we thought were ours alone.

This is not the poetry of facile inspiration or easy uplift. But reading these poems, one feels less alone, in the presence of someone who is marvelously good at paying attention, and who has the gift to articulate previously unnoticed aspects of experience. As the speaker of "Ocracoke" affirms: "The deeper the listening, / the richer the world." In *Into the Good World Again*, Max Garland opens up a rich world indeed.

CHRISTOPHER BOUCHER

SMELL THE WORDS™

People have been adding smells to literature for years, but it wasn't until 2022 that the trend really took hold. All the big books published that year—*Cordelia's Hat, Nice/Not Nice, Kalamazoo, Salad Apostrophe*—were sold in "aromatic editions" that featured "smellpoints" at which, upon a page turn or retinal reading confirmation, a relevant smell would be emitted via tiny wires running through the pages and connecting back to a proprietary chemical cartridge system in the book's spine. In the climactic scene of *Apostrophe,* for example, the anti-anti heroine Moire DeNaught holds up her salad in defiance and shouts, "Make mine a *Caesar!*" When those words were read in the aromatic edition, a chemical spritz made the air above the page *smell* like a Caesar Salad.

While the technology was expensive and time-consuming—it involved the installation of hundreds of miniature pex tubes, a power source (usually solar), and a governing computer that managed the reading sensors and dispersion of chemicals— aromatic literature, or "smelly books," completely revitalized the industry. Thirty-five percent of books sold across the world that year were smelly. The annual Bookies even created a new category to recognize them: Bix Dalv's *Forever Breakfast* won the first-ever Bookie for Best Aromatic Literature of 2022.

It wasn't long before literary journals got in on the craze, too. In February 2023, *The Worcester Review* included one aromatic poem, L. D. Forest's "Ocean Avenue," in their spring issue. *Guffaw* followed in April with a smell-forward essay called "A Meditation on Traffic," by Rose Mustang. Soon, every journal worth the smell of salt was adding scents to their pages.

Exacting Clam began making plans to publish their first smelly issue in the winter of 2024. I was in the editorial suite when Smell the Words™, a local literary aromatic installer, pitched us for the bid to aromatize the next issue. The husband-and-wife team seemed knowledgeable and personable, but I was appalled at the figures they quoted us. Ten thousand dollars to run the lines? Eight K more for the chemicals? Halfway through the pitch I leaned over to Emily Why, another editor at *Clam*, and said, "Couldn't we do this ourselves?"

"Which part?" she hissed.

"All this stuff's available online. You run a power source, connect your lines to the smell spots, and voila!"

"I don't know," Why whispered. "Seems pretty complicated to me."

When I pitched this idea to the full editorial board, others were skeptical as well. "There's a lot involved here, Boucher," said Mar Doyle, leaning over the table. "What do you know about installing a power source?"

"I'm pretty sure it's just a basic solar generator," I said.

"But what about the scents themselves?" said my colleague Sigh from across the room.

"Can't we just buy a basic aroma package and mix any smells we don't have?"

Sigh looked to Why, who shrugged.

"And you'd oversee this?" said Doyle.

"Absolutely," I said. "I'll take care of the whole thing."

The board gave me the go-ahead and I got to work. Issue 13 was particularly smell-heavy – what with the odors of socks in the review "Into the Good World Again," wood-paneled walls and a jar of roses in "Mountain Spirit," and gargantuan frogs, darkness and octopi (not to mention a *whale*!) in "Breath-taking"—so I began by making a comprehensive list of smells and extensive notes about how I'd achieve each. Some bouquets were straightforward, but for others I had to draw on everything I'd ever known about odor and language. I created the smell of ennui by mixing the essence of filing cabinets with the scent of crumbling sidewalks. For worry I went with pongs of perspiration, one part electricity, and the waft of something spoiled. To create the "inverse relationship between proximity and access" I mixed two cups' silence, the fragrance of longing and the whiff an of an open field.

I ran into plenty of challenges, though. Have you ever tried running mini-pex wires through an entire issue of a literary journal? It's not as easy it sounds; I bungled four of my first five connections, and kept confusing one line with another. When we held a full-issue smell-through later that month, the odor of old t-shirts in "n+1 and other modes" was overwhelming—while none of the smells in "Smog Mammoth" worked at all! I'd mistakenly reversed the smells of a butterfly and sorrows in "Into the Good World Again," and then it turned out that Why had a sensitivity to the honeysuckle odor in "Mountain Spirit"—a sensitivity she'd informed us of repeatedly, she reminded us before storming off the page. As she did so, the entire system suddenly lost power. I was resetting the computer when I felt a hand on my shoulder and turned around to see Sigh standing behind me with a grim expression on his face. "This just isn't working, Chris," he said.

"I'll have the power back on in five," I said, "and then I just need to recrimp these connections—"

"No," said Becker. "We're going to have to go a different way here."

That afternoon, the editors held an emergency meeting at which they decided to remove me from the project and reach out to Smell the Books™ to inquire about salvaging the issue. But STB was booked through August, and they wouldn't sign on unless we paid extra to remove everything I'd done and re-aromatize from scratch. Given our sunk costs and the threat of a six-month production delay, the editors decided to publish Issue 13 without smells.

Looking back, though, that was probably for the best. Not long afterwards, smelly books began to fade in popularity. That fall, in fact, a backlash (#mybooksdontsmell) began online and sales of aromatic editions fell considerably. Nowadays, you hardly ever see a smelly book anymore.

But you know what? I think literature already *has* a smell. Here—lean down to the page and take a whiff. Go ahead—breathe it in. See? Doesn't the language already pong of old roses and trying; the spine of glue and sorrow; the page itself of proximity, hope and tomorrow?

Iván Argüelles

Fattening Frogs for Snakes

the corpse's name was McDermott
dressed in a white shirt suit and tie
just like they were this anonymous
hot summer afternoon after the rites
went and sat on the terraced hill
behind the hospital where they were
born to meditate upon death all
a-sweat in formal gear musing upon
the imponderable the gilded tomb
the ethereal silence what it was and
was not the immense imperial sky
endless azure cloudless odor of grass
leaning west noise like tinker toys
from afar car horns brakes asphalt
whatever remains of the moment
only a year older why was he dead ?
ultimately will everything burn to a crisp ?
turn the mind if possible to other
matters rhythm 'n blues song titles
how evening needs no preparation
about the alcohol to be consumed
hidden contents of bottles and letters
a Latin structure to syntax the air
itself layers of invisible archaeology
resounding with unseen inscriptions
taken from the Parthenon in a dream
whittled a small omicron out of bark
smelled the distant diesel fumes traffic
all heading for hell and the corpse
fresh in its timber box the outline of
destiny a blur father was a sports coach
burly ill-mannered no nonsense Jack
of a guy snickered thinking of his gravity
an incapacity to fly to levitate to raise
a thought to the gods who took him away
sun slowly setting over a parchment
called time and getting up slightly
drunk wend the passage home trees
and a holy remoteness to everything
Fattening frogs for snakes   *3-19-24*

Contributors

Iván Argüelles (1939–2024) was an innovative and prolific Mexican-American poet. Sagging Meniscus was honored to publish two of his many (more than 50) collections, *The Rudiments of Poetry* and *The Blank Page*. "Fattening Frogs for Snakes" is the last poem he sent us.

Stephen Bett is a widely and internationally published Canadian poet with 24 books in print, & with a new book, *Broken Glosa: an alphabet book of post-avant glosa*, coming out shortly with Chax Press. His personal papers are archived in the "Contemporary Literature Collection" at Simon Fraser University.

P.J. Blumenthal, an American writer in Munich, Germany, writes in both German and English. He is the author of a non-fiction book on feral man, *Kaspar Hausers Geschwister* (Kaspar Hauser's Siblings), and the novel *Winston Hewlett's Impotence* (SM, 2024).

Tori Bond is a screenwriter, playwright and the author of *Familyism* (Matter Press, 2019), a collection of flash fiction. Her work has appeared in *McSweeney's Internet Tendency, Monkeybicycle, Atticus Review, Flash Fiction Funny* anthology, and others. She received an MFA in Creative Writing from Rosemont College and studied comedy writing at The Second City.

Christopher Boucher is the author of the novels *How to Keep Your Volkswagen Alive* (Melville House, 2011), *Golden Delicious* (MH, 2016), and *Big Giant Floating Head* (MH, 2019). He teaches writing and literature at Boston College and is Managing Editor of *Post Road Magazine*.

Samson Bulkley's work has also appeared in *Add To Cart Magazine*.

Marvin Cohen is the author of many novels, plays, and collections of essays, stories, and poems, most recently *How, Upon Reflection, To Be Amorous* (SM, 2023). He lives in Manhattan.

Bradley David's poetry, fiction, essays, images, and genre-bending work appears in *Terrain, Allium, Rougarou, Exacting Clam, Always Crashing, Anti-Heroin Chic, Identity Theory*, and numerous other publications. He is a Pushcart Prize nominee and senior editor at *JMWW*.

T.K. Edmond is a Fort Worth, Texas writer, musician, SweeTart, and screwup. T.K. is interested in dramaturgy, beauty and cruelty colliding in Texas, and conceptualism. Recent work can be found in *ZiNDaily, Abridged, Coffin Bell, Pidgeonholes*, and soon in *Apocalypse Confidential*.

Andrew Farkas is the author of *The Great Indoorsman: Essays, The Big Red Herring, Sunsphere*, and the forthcoming *Are You Now, or Have You Ever Been?* He is Associate Professor of Creative Writing at Washburn University and an editor for *Always Crashing*.

Fred Ferraris' work has been published in periodicals, including *Bombay Gin, Cafe Irreal, Cold Mountain Review, Orbis, Stand*, and *The Worcester Review*, in the anthologies *Prayers For A Thousand Years* (HarperSanFrancisco) and *Ginosko Anthology 2* (MadHat Press), the chapbooks *Marpa Point* (Blackberry) and *The Durango Chronicles* (Blue Marmot Press), and a full-length book, *Older Than Rain* (Selva Editions).

S.C. Flynn was born in a small town in Australia of Irish origin and now lives in Dublin. His poetry has been published in many magazines and in March 2023, leading US magazine *Rattle* included him as one of seventeen contemporary Irish poets in a special edition. In May 2023 he was long-listed for the Erbacce Prize.

Jack Foley's numerous books of poetry, fiction and criticism include *Visions and Affiliations*, a "chronoencyclopedia" of California poetry from 1940 to 2005, *Grief Songs* (SM, 2017) and *When Sleep Comes* (SM, 2020). He lives in Oakland and hosts a weekly radio show, *Cover to Cover*, on Berkeley's Pacifica station, KPFA.

Olivia Gallo was born in Buenos Aires, Argentina, in 1995. Her novel *No son vacaciones* (2023) was recently published by Blatt & Rios, a short story collection, *Las chicas no lloran*, was published by Tenemos las Máquinas (Argentina) in 2019 and Alpha

Decay (Spain) in 2022 and a collection of pandemic correspondence with the writer Tamara Talesnik, *Intranquilas & Venenosas*, was published by Odelia (Argentina) in 2021. She has run a creative writing workshop since 2021.

Jake Goldsmith is a writer with cystic fibrosis and the founder of The Barbellion Prize, a book prize for ill and disabled authors. He is the author of *Neither Weak Nor Obtuse* (SM, 2022) and *In Hospital Environments: Essays on Illness and Philosophy* (SM, 2024).

Tyler C. Gore's essays, stories, and reviews have appeared in many of the fine, high-quality journals preferred by discerning readers like you. He is the author of *My Life of Crime: Essays and Other Entertainments* (SM, 2022), a delightful book that you should definitely buy. He lives, as he dreams, in Brooklyn.

AN Grace lives in Liverpool, England. His work has appeared or is forthcoming in *Queen's Quarterly, Seize The Press, Menacing Hedge, Fantasy & Science Fiction* and others.

Oisín Harris is a working class poet. His poems have appeared in *The Denver Quarterly, The Moth, The Sublunary Review*, and elsewhere. He has contributed a chapter entitled "Women in Translation and Contributing Reasons of Underrepresentation" in the eBook *Translating Women in the Anglosphere: Activism in Action*.

Charles Holdefer lives in Brussels. He is the author of *Don't Look at Me*, a novel about Emily Dickinson, basketball, and the persistence of literature in a post-literary world (SM, 2022). His next book is a forthcoming collection of stories, *Ivan the Terrible Goes on a Family Picnic* (SM, 2024).

Richard Kostelanetz is an American writer, artist, critic, and editor of the avant-garde. He survives in New York, where he was born, unemployed and thus overworked.

Roy Lisker (1938–2019) was a writer, artist, mathematician, journalist and political activist. He was the author of a vast amount of literature in every imaginable form, which he largely self-distributed to friends and subscribers to his newsletter, *Ferment*. His conventionally published work includes *In Memoriam Einstein* (SM, 2016) and *Lincoln Center in July* (SM, 2016).

Kurt Luchs' most recent book is *Death Row Row Row Your Boat* (SM, 2024). He lives in Michigan.

Kit Maude is a translator based in Buenos Aires. He has translated dozens of Latin American writers for a wide array of publications and writes reviews for *Ñ, Otra Parte*, and the *Times Literary Supplement*.

David Rose was born in 1949. He has published two novels—*Vault* and *Meridian*—and two story collections—*Posthumous Stories* and *Interpolated Stories*. He appears in *The Penguin Book of the Contemporary British Short Story* (ed. Hensher).

George Salis is the author of the novels *Sea Above, Sun Below* and *Morphological Echoes*. He edits *The Collidescope*, an online publication that celebrates innovative and neglected literature. He has taught in Bulgaria, China, and Poland. He's the winner of the Tom La Farge Award for Innovative Writing.

Shya Scanlon is the author of the novel *The Guild of Saint Cooper* and the poetry collection *In This Alone Impulse*. His stories and nonfiction have been published widely but sporadically. He lives in upstate New York with his wife and their dog.

Marcus Silcock (formerly Slease) is a surreal-absurd poet from Portadown, N. Ireland. He is the co-editor of the surreal-absurd sampler at *Mercurius* magazine. His latest books are *Puppy, Never Mind the Beasts*, and *The Green Monk*.

Mike Silverton is the author of *Anvil on a Shoestring* (SM, 2022), *Trios* (SM, 2023) and *Yoga for Pickpockets* (SM, 2024). He lives in Maine.

Lucian Staiano-Daniels is a historian of violent conflict who was educated at St. John's College, NYU, and UCLA.

Thomas Walton is the author of *Good Morning Bone Crusher!* (Spuyten Duyvil 2021), *All the Useless Things Are Mine* (SM, 2020), *The World Is All That Does Befall Us* (Ravenna Press, 2019), and, with Elizabeth Cooperman, *The Last Mosaic* (SM, 2018). He currently works as an AI yoga instructor at Ashram Deapphake in Seattle, WA.

www.ingramcontent.com/pod-product-compliance
Lightning Source LLC
Chambersburg PA
CBHW081326020726

47506CB00006B/1197